Level Up! Lebanese Arabic Stories

Book 1

lingualism

ISBN: 978-1-962752-08-4

Written by Sarah Khoury

Edited by Charbel Ghaleb and Matthew Aldrich

Audio by Charbel Ghaleb

website: www.lingualism.com

email: contact@lingualism.com

Table of Contents

Introduction

Welcome to "Level Up!", a unique approach to reading in Lebanese Arabic. This series is designed specifically for adult learners, offering culturally authentic stories that explore Lebanese life, history, and traditions. Each book in the series contains six original stories, with every story presented in four versions corresponding to CEFR levels A1 through B2.

The innovative format of "Level Up!" emerged from learner feedback on our "One Thousand and One Nights" series, where readers who purchased both elementary and intermediate books found that reading the elementary version helped them build confidence and skills to tackle the intermediate version. This led us to develop a new approach: presenting all four versions of each story together, allowing learners to experience how complexity builds naturally while maintaining the same core narrative.

Why is this approach effective? When you read the A1 version of a story first, regardless of your current level, you build a strong foundation of basic vocabulary and story comprehension. As you progress through the versions, you'll recognize familiar elements while encountering new vocabulary and more complex structures gradually rather than feeling overwhelmed by them all at once.

Each story in this collection has been carefully crafted to reflect authentic Lebanese experiences and perspectives. From modern life in Beirut to historical backdrops like the French Mandate, these stories provide not just language practice but also deep cultural insights. The adult-oriented themes ensure that the content remains engaging and relevant to mature learners.

Throughout the book, you'll find helpful features to support your learning journey. Before each story group, an Introduction provides cultural context, followed by Key Vocabulary that you'll encounter across the different versions. Every story has also been recorded by a native Lebanese voice artist, with slower, clearer pronunciation for A1/A2 versions and more natural pacing for B1/B2.

How to Use This Book

The unique format of "Level Up!" has been carefully designed to support your learning journey. Here's how to make the most of its features:

Story Versions and Layout

Each story appears in four versions, with layouts specifically designed for different learning needs. All versions include voweling marks (tashkeel) on the Arabic text, using a simplified system that omits the fatha where it can be easily predicted, reducing visual clutter while maintaining readability.

A1 Version:

- o Three-column format (Arabic script, phonemic transcription, English translation)
- o The phonemic transcription helps beginners connect sounds to script
- o Short, simple sentences with basic vocabulary

A2 Version:

- o Two-column format (Arabic and English only)
- o Phonemic transcription is removed to encourage direct reading of Arabic
- o Slightly longer sentences with expanded vocabulary

B1 Version:

- o Single-column format with English following each paragraph
- o More complex sentence structures
- o Quick reference to translation while maintaining focus on Arabic

B2 Version:

- Arabic text with English on following page
- Most complex structures and vocabulary
- Translation placement encourages independent reading

Reading Strategy

We recommend starting with the A1 version of each story, regardless of your current level. This approach helps you:

- Build confidence with the basic narrative
- Establish core vocabulary
- Recognize story elements that will appear in higher levels
- Progress naturally to more complex versions when ready

Vocabulary and Cultural Notes

- Before each story group, you'll find:
- An Introduction providing cultural context
- Key Vocabulary listing important words and expressions
- These sections help prepare you for all versions of the story

Audio Recordings

Each version has been recorded by a native Lebanese voice artist:

- A1/A2 recordings are slower and clearer, with appropriate pauses
- B1/B2 recordings maintain clarity while using more natural pacing
- Use recordings to practice listening comprehension and pronunciation

- Listen while reading to reinforce learning

Remember, the goal is to read for pleasure and understanding. Don't feel pressured to move to a higher level version until you're comfortable. Each version offers valuable learning opportunities, and the familiar content helps you focus on new language features as they're introduced.

Visit www.lingualism.com/audio, where you can find the free accompanying audio to download or stream (at variable playback rates).

البيْت المُشْترك

The Shared House

In a time when Lebanese families are increasingly scattered across continents, three cousins inherit their سِتّ *sitt* (grandmother)'s بيْت عتيق *bēt 3atī?* (traditional house) in جْبَيْل *jbayl* (Byblos). Through weekly meetings on Zoom and shared ذِكْرَيات *zikrayēt* (memories), they discover that their grandmother's تُراث *turās* (heritage) – from her handwritten وَصْفات *waṣfēt* (recipes) to her beloved شجْرِةْ التّين *šájrit ittīn* (fig tree) - might hold the key to keeping their family connected across oceans. Can they transform this silent house into a place that bridges past and present, while preserving its soul for future generations?

Key Vocabulary

- بالْكوْن (*balkōn*) – balcony
- برّا (*bárra*) – abroad
- بيْت ضْيافِة (*bēt ḍyāfi*) – guesthouse
- ترْويقة (*tarwīʔa*) – breakfast
- تِصْليح (*tiṣlīḥ*) – repair
- جْذور (*jzūr*) – roots
- جْنَيْنِة (*jnáyni*) – garden
- حنين (*ḥanīn*) – nostalgia
- سِتّ (*sitt*) – grandmother
- ضْيوف (*ḍyūf*) – guests
- عَيْلِة (*3áyli*)– family
- مشْروع (*mašrū3*) – project
- مهْجر (*máhjar*) – diaspora
- مونِة (*mūni*) – preserved food
- يَوْمِيّات (*yawmiyyēt*) – diary

A1

The Shared House	*-lbēt ilmúštarak*	البيْت المُشْترك
Sitt (Grandma) Nada left a big house in Byblos. The house became her grandchildren's.	*sitt náda tárakit bēt kbīr bi-jbēl. -lbēt ṣār la-wlēd wlēda.*	سِتّ ندى تركت بيْت كْبير بِجْبيْل. البيْت صار لَوْلاد وْلادا.
Wissam lives in Lebanon. Yumna lives in America. Ziad lives in Abu Dhabi.	*wisām 3āyiš bi-libnēn. yúmna 3āyši bi-ʔamērka. ziyād 3āyiš bi-ʔábu ẓábi.*	وِسام عايِش بِلِبْنان. يُمْنى عايْشِة بِأميْركا. زِياد عايِش بِأبو ظبي.
Every Friday, they talk together on the computer. They talk about the house.	*kill júm3a, byíħku ma3 ba3ḍ 3a -lkōmbyūtir. byíħku 3an ilbēt.*	كِلّ جُمْعة، بْيِحْكوا مع بعْض عَ الكومْبْيوتِر. بْيِحْكوا عن البيْت.
Wissam said, "The house is old and needs repair."	*wisām ʔāl: "-lbēt ʔadīm u báddu tiṣlīħ.*	وِسام قال: "البيْت قديم وبدّو تِصْليح.
Yumna said, "We won't sell it. This is our grandmother's house!"	*yúmna ʔālit: "ma baddna nbī3u. háyda bēt síttna!"*	يُمْنى قالِت: "ما بدّْنا نْبيعو. هَيْدا بيْت سِتّْنا!"

Ziad said, “Let’s make it a guesthouse.”	*ziyād ʔāl: “xallīna ná3imlu bēt ḍyāfi.”*	زِياد قال: "خلّينا نعِمْلو بيْت ضْيافِة."
They fixed the house together. Wissam supervised the work. Yumna chose the furniture. Ziad made a plan for the project.	*ṣállaɧu -lbēt sáwa. wisām šáraf 3ála -ššíɣil. yúmna xtārit ilʔasēs. ziyād 3ímil xíṭṭa la-lmašrū3.*	صلّحو البيْت سَوا. وِسام شرف على الشِّغِل. يُمْنى خْتارِت الأثاث. زِياد عِمِل خِطّة لَلْمشْروع.
Now the house is beautiful. There are guests every day. They drink coffee under the fig tree.	*hállaʔ ilbēt ṣār ɧílu. fī ḍyūf kill yōm. byíšrabu ʔáhwi táɧit šájrit ittīn.*	هلّأ البيْت صار حِلو. في ضْيوف كِلّ يوْم. بْيِشْربوا قهْوِة تحِت شجْرِة التّين.
Most importantly, the family talks to each other every week.	*w-ilʔahámm, -l3áyli ṣārit tíɧki ma3 bá3ḍa kill ʔusbū3.*	والأهمّ، العَيْلِة صارِت تِحْكي مع بعْضا كِلّ أُسْبوع.

The Shared House | البيْت المُشْترك

“The house is big, and the view is beautiful, but no one can live in it now.”	”البيْت كْبير، والمنْظر حِلو، بسّ ما في يِسْكُن حدا هلّأ.“
Wissam is explaining to his cousins over Zoom. He’s the only one in Lebanon, looking at their grandmother’s house in Byblos.	وِسام عم يِشْرح لَوْلاد عمّو عبِر تِطْبيق زوم. هُوِّ الوَحيد يَلّي بِلِبْنان، وعم يِتْطلّع على بيْت سِتُّن بِجْبيْل.
Yumna, who lives in Michigan, is taking notes. “How’s the main bedroom?”	يُمْنى، يَلّي عايْشِة بِميشيغان، عم تِكْتُب مُلاحظات. ”كيف أوْضِةْ النّوْم الرّئيسية؟“
“There are three bedrooms, all with problems. The roof needs repair, and the electricity is old.”	”في تْلات أُوَض نوْم، كِلُّن فِيُن مشاكِل. السّقِف بدّو تِصْليح، والكهْربا قديمِة.“
Ziad, their cousin who lives in Abu Dhabi, asked, “What are we going to do with it?”	زِياد، اِبْن عمُّن يَلّي عايِش بِأبو ظبي، سأل: ”شو رح نعْمُل فيه؟“
Their grandmother Nada’s house became theirs after she passed away. She was the last person to live in it.	بيْت سِتُّن ندى صار مِلْكُن بعِد ما تْوَفِّت. هِيِّ كانِت آخِر حدا ساكِن فيه.

"I have an idea," said Yumna. "Why don't we fix it and make it a guesthouse?"	"عِنْدي فِكْرة،" قالِت يُمْنى. "لَيْش ما مِنْصلْحو ومْنعِمْلو بيْت ضْيافِة؟"
"But who will manage it?" asked Ziad.	"بسّ مين رح يْديرو؟" سأل زِياد.
"I'm here," said Wissam. "I can monitor it and check its work."	"أنا هوْن،" قال وِسام. "فِيّي راقْبو وشوف شِغْلو."
They decided to share the expenses. Ziad pays for the roof repair, Yumna takes care of decoration, and Wissam supervises the work.	قرّروا يِتْشاركوا المصاريف. زِياد بْيِدْفع تِصْليح السّقِف، يُمْنى بْتِهْتمّ بِالدّيكوْر، ووِسام بْيِشْرُف على الشِّغِل.
Every Friday, they have a Zoom meeting. Wissam photographs the house and shows them what's happening.	كِلّ يوْم جُمْعة، بْيعِمْلوا إجْتِماع عَ الزّوم. وِسام بيصوِّر البيْت وبيفرْجِيْن شو عم بيصير.
"Look what I found!" said Wissam on Friday. He lifted an old box. "This is Sitt Nada's box. It has old photos and antique things."	"شوفوا شو لْقيت!" قال وِسام يوْم الجُمْعة. شال صنْدوق قديم. "هَيْدا صنْدوق سِتّ ندى. في صُوَر قديمِة وإشْيا عتيقة."
"You know what?" said Yumna. "This house brought us together again. We don't see each other much, but now we talk every week!"	"بْتعِرْفوا؟" قالِت يُمْنى. "هَيْدا البيْت جمعْنا مِن جْديد. نِحْنا ما مِنْشوف بعْض كْتير، بسّ هلّأ عم نِحْكي كِلّ أُسْبوع!"

البيْت المُشْترك

The Shared House

"مُسْتحيل نْبيعو! هَيْدا بيْت سِتّي!"

"Impossible to sell it! This is my grandmother's house!"

صوْت يُمْنى كان واضِح عبر الزّوم، مع إنّا بِبَيْتا بِميشيغان، آلاف الكيلومِتْرات بْعيدِة عن لِبْنان.

Yumna's voice was clear over Zoom, even though she was at her home in Michigan, thousands of kilometers away from Lebanon.

"بسّ يا يُمْنى،" قال زِياد مِن أبو ظبي، "البيْت بدّو مصاري كْتير. السّقِف، الكهْربا، السّنْغرية... كِلّو خِرْبان."

"But Yumna," said Ziad from Abu Dhabi, "the house needs a lot of money. The roof, electricity, plumbing... everything's broken."

وِسام، يَلّي كان واقِف بِبيْت سِتُّن ندى بِجْبيْل، فتح الكاميرا على المطْبخ القديم. "شوفوا... البْلاط الأزْرق يَلّي سِتّ ندى كانِت تْحِبّو بعْدو مَوْجود. والطّاوْلِة يَلّي كِنّا نِتْرَوّق عْلَيا كِلّ صيْف..."

Wissam, who was standing in their grandmother Nada's house in Byblos, turned the camera to the old kitchen. "Look... the blue tiles that Sitt Nada loved are still here. And the table where we had breakfast every summer..."

سكتوا تْلاتِتُن. كِلّ واحد عم يِتْذكّر صيْفِيّات مِخْتِلْفِة بِبيْت سِتُّن. يُمْنى تْذكّرِت ريحِةْ القهْوِة الصُّبُح. زِياد تْذكّر اللَّيالي يَلّي كانوا يِلْعبوا فِيا

وَرق على البالْكوْن. ووِسام تْذكّر سِتّ ندى هِيِّ وعم تْعلِّمْن يعِمْلوا مْربّى التّين.

All three fell silent. Each one remembering different summers in their grandmother's house. Yumna remembered the smell of morning coffee. Ziad remembered the nights they played cards on the balcony. And Wissam remembered Sitt Nada teaching them how to make fig jam.

"عِنْدي فِكْرة،" قالِت يُمْنى. "ليْش ما مِنْحَوْلوا لبيْت ضْيافِة؟ نْصلِّحو ونْخلّي النّاس تْعيش نفْس الجّوّ يَلّي عِشْنا."

"I have an idea," said Yumna. "Why don't we turn it into a guesthouse? We'll fix it and let people experience the same atmosphere we lived in."

"فِكْرة حِلْوِة،" قال وِسام. "بسّ مين رح يْدير المشْروع؟"

"Nice idea," said Wissam. "But who will manage the project?"

"كِلّنا!" قالِت يُمْنى بِحماس. "إنْتَ بْتِشْرُف على الشِّغِل لِأنّك بِلِبْنان. أنا بْصمِّم الدّيْكوْر وبعْمِل صفْحات السّوشْيال ميدْيا. وزِياد عِنْدو خِبْرة بِالْفنادِق، فِيو يَعْمُل خِطّة عمل."

"All of us!" Yumna said enthusiastically. "You supervise the work since you're in Lebanon. I'll design the decor and create social media pages. And Ziad has hotel experience, he can make the business plan."

زِياد فكّر شْوَيّ. "طيِّب، بسّ لازِم نْقسِّم المْصاريف. أنا بِدْفع تِصْليح السّقِف والكهْربا."

Ziad thought for a moment. "Okay, but we need to divide the expenses. I'll pay for fixing the roof and electricity."

"وأنا بْجيب الفرِش والدّيكور،" قالِت يُمْنى.

"And I'll get the furniture and decor," said Yumna.

"وأنا بِشرُف على العِمّال وبِخْتار المَوادّ،" قال وِسام.

"And I'll supervise the workers and choose the materials," said Wissam.

وهيْك بلّشِت الرِّحْلِة. كِلّ جُمْعة، بْيِجْتِمْعوا عَ الزّوم يْشوفوا التّقدُّم. وِسام كان يْصوِّر كِلّ التّفاصيل: العِمّال عم يْصلْحوا السّقِف، الكهْرَبْجي عم يْمِدّ أسْلاك جْديدِة، النّجار عم يْرمِّم الخزايِن العتيقة.

And so the journey began. Every Friday, they met on Zoom to see the progress. Wissam would photograph all the details: workers fixing the roof, the electrician installing new wires, the carpenter restoring old cabinets.

يوْم الجُمْعة، وِسام فتح صنْدوق قديم لاقا بِالْعِلّية.

One Friday, Wissam opened an old box he found in the attic.

"شو هَيْدا؟" سألِت يُمْنى.

"What's that?" asked Yumna.

"صنْدوق سِتّ ندى. في..." وِسام سكت. "في دفْتر يَوْمِيّات!"

"Sitt Nada's box. It has..." Wissam paused. "It has a diary!"

"قْري شي مِنّو!" قال زِياد.

"Read something from it!" said Ziad.

فتح وِسام الدّفْتر وبلّش يِقْرا: "اليوْم زرعِت شجْرةْ تين بِالْحديقة. انْشالله وْلادي ووْلاد وْلادي رح ياكْلوا مِن تيناتا..."

Wissam opened the diary and started reading. “Today I planted a fig tree in the garden. God willing, my children and grandchildren will eat from its figs...”

دمّعِت عيْن يُمْنى. “شجْرِةْ التّين بعْدا مَوْجودِة؟”

Yumna’s eyes welled up. “Is the fig tree still there?”

“أيْ،” قال وِسام. “وبعْدا بْتعْطي. بسّ ما حدا عم يْلِمّ التّين مِن سْنين...”

“Yes,” said Wissam. “And it still bears fruit. But no one has picked the figs for years...”

“بْتعِرْفوا شو؟” قال زِياد. “خلّينا نْخلّي كِلّ شي مِتِل ما هُوِّ. نْصلّح يَلّي لازِم، بسّ نْحافِظ على روح البيْت.”

“You know what?” said Ziad. “Let’s keep everything as it is. Fix what’s necessary, but preserve the spirit of the house.”

مرقِت الأسابيع. البيْت بلّش يْتِغيّر، بسّ بِطريقة حِلْوِة. يُمْنى خْتارِت فرِش بيناسِب الطِّراز القديم. زِياد عِمِل مَوْقع إلِكْتْرونْي للْبيْت، وحطّ صُوَر قديمِة وجْديدِة. ووِسام رتّب الحديقة وزرع ورِد حَوْل شجْرِةْ التّين.

Weeks passed. The house started to change, but in a beautiful way. Yumna chose furniture that matched the old style. Ziad created a website for the house, putting up old and new photos. And Wissam arranged the garden and planted flowers around the fig tree.

“بدّْنا نِخْتار إسِم للْمشْروع،” قالِت يُمْنى.

“We need to choose a name for the project,” said Yumna.

"بيْت سِتّ ندى؟" قْترح وِسام.

"Sitt Nada's House?" suggested Wissam.

"حِلو... بسّ في شي أحْلى،" قالِت يُمْنى. "خلّينا نْسمّيه: بيْت التّين."

"Nice... but there's something better," said Yumna. "Let's call it: The Fig House."

"ليْه؟"

"Why?"

"لِأنّو مِتِل شجْرِةْ التّين. جُذورو عميقة، وكِلّ سِنة بْيَعْطي مِن جْديد."

"Because it's like the fig tree. Its roots are deep, and every year it bears fruit again."

بعِد سِتِّة شْهور، سْتقْبل البيْت أوّل ضْيوفو. عَيْلِة لِبْنانية مِن المهْجر، مِتِل يُمْنى وزِياد، جايّين يْعيشوا تجْرِبِةْ البيْت اللِّبْناني القديم.

After six months, the house welcomed its first guests. A Lebanese family from abroad, like Yumna and Ziad, coming to experience life in an old Lebanese house.

يُمْنى صارِت تْشوف التّعْليقات على المَوْقع كِلّ يوْم: "حسّيْنا حالْنا بِبيْت سِتّْنا"... "التّرْويقة عَ البالْكوْن شي خيالي"... "شجْرِةْ التّين عم تْذكِّرْنا بِبْيوت ضَيْعِتْنا..."

Yumna started reading the website comments daily. "We felt like we were in our grandmother's house"... "Breakfast on the balcony was magical"... "The fig tree reminded us of our village homes..."

بسّ أحْلى تِعْليق كان مِن سِتّ كْبيرِة بِالْعُمُر: "هَيْدا البيْت زبط معي. كِنِت عم دوِّر على محلّ يْذكِّرْني بِبيْت أهْلي."

But the nicest comment was from an elderly lady. “This house suited me perfectly. I was looking for a place that would remind me of my family home.”

صار البيْت نِقْطِةْ لقاء. الضِّيوف بْيِحْكوا مع بعْض، بْيِتْبادلوا قِصص، بْيِشْربوا قهْوِةْ الصُّبُح تحِت شجْرِةْ التّين.

The house became a meeting point. Guests talk with each other, exchange stories, drink morning coffee under the fig tree.

وكِلّ جُمْعة، بْيِجْتِمْعوا يُمْنى وزِياد ووِسام عَ الزّوم. ما عاد يِحْكوا بسّ عن شِغِل البيْت. صاروا يِحْكوا عن حَياتُن، عن وْلادُن، عن أحْلامُن.

And every Friday, Yumna, Ziad, and Wissam meet on Zoom. They no longer just talk about the house work. They talk about their lives, their children, their dreams.

"بْتعِرْفوا؟" قال وِسام. "سِتّ ندى كان عِنْدا حقّ. البيْت مِش حيْطان وسقِف. البيْت قِصص وذِكْرَيات. ونِحْنا هلّأ عم نعْمُل قِصص جْديدِة."

“You know?” said Wissam. “Sitt Nada was right. A house isn’t just walls and a roof. It’s stories and memories. And now we’re making new stories.”

البيْت المُشْترك

"هَيْدا مِش قرار مْنِقْدر ناخْدوا بِدْقيقْتيْن عَ زوم... هَيْدي قُطْعة مِن تاريخْنا."

يُمْنى تْنهّدِت وهِيِّ عم تِشْرب قهْوِتا بِميشيغان. السّاعة عِنْدا ستِّة الصُّبْح، بسّ ما كان في مجال تْأجِّل الإجْتِماع. بِالنِّسْبِة لزِياد بِأبو ظبي، كان بعِد الضُّهُر، ووِسام بِبيْت سِتُّن بِجْبيْل كان عم يْشوف آخِر شُعاع شمْس عم يِلْعب على البْلاط القديم.

"بسّ يُمْنى، شو المنْطِق نِصْرُف مصاري على بيْت ما حدا رح يِسْكُن فيه؟" سأل زِياد. كمُدير فنادِق، كان دايْماً بيفكِّر بِالْأرْقام. "مِنْبيعوه، ومِنْقسِّم المصاري..."

"مصاري؟" قاطعِتو. "إنْتَ بْتِتْذكّر لمّا كِنّا نِتْخبّى وَرا البرادي القديمِة ونِلْعب غمّيضة؟ بْتِتْذكّر ريحِةْ الياسْمين يَلّي زرعْتو سِتّ ندى؟ هَيْدوْل ما إلُن سِعِر."

وِسام، يَلّي كان ساكِت مِن أوّل الإجْتِماع، مِشي للْبالْكوْن. الكاميرا تبعو صوّرِت المنْظر: جْبال لِبْنان بِالبْعيد، وبِالْقُرْب شجْرِةْ التّين العتيقة يَلّي زرعِتا سِتُّن.

"بْتعِرْفوا شو قْريت بِدفْتر يَوْمِيّاتا؟" قال فجْأة. "كتبِت: 'البيْت روح العَيْلِة. ما بيموت إلّا إذا نْسينا.'"

"شو قصْدك؟" سأل زِياد.

The Shared House

"This isn't a decision we can make in two minutes on Zoom... this is a piece of our history."

Yumna sighed as she drank her coffee in Michigan. It was six in the morning for her, but the meeting couldn't be postponed. For Ziad in Abu Dhabi, it was afternoon, and Wissam in their grandmother's house in Byblos was watching the last ray of sunlight playing on the old tiles.

"But Yumna, what's the logic in spending money on a house no one will live in?" asked Ziad. As a hotel manager, he always thought in numbers. "Let's sell it, and split the money..."

"Money?" she interrupted. "Do you remember when we used to hide behind the old curtains and play hide and seek? Do you remember the smell of jasmine that Sitt Nada planted? These things don't have a price."

Wissam, who had been quiet since the start of the meeting, walked to the balcony. His camera captured the view: Lebanon's mountains in the distance, and nearby, the ancient fig tree their grandmother had planted.

"Do you know what I read in her diary?" he said suddenly. "She wrote: 'The house is the family's soul. It only dies if we forget it.'"

"What do you mean?" asked Ziad.

"قصْدي... يِمْكِن في حل وسط. ما نْبيعو، وما نْخلّي يِخْرب. نِحْييه مِن جْديد."

فتح وِسام الكاميرا على صفْحة مِن دفْتر سِتّ ندى: "بَيْتْنا صار محطّة. كِلّ صيْف بْيِرْجعوا وْلادي مِن برّا، وبيجيبوا معُن حْكايات جْديدِة. وكِلّ شي بْيِحْكوا بيصير جِزء مِن حيْطان البيْت."

"عِنْدي فِكْرة،" قالِت يُمْنى. عْيونا كانِت عم تِلْمع رغْم التّعب. "خلّيْنا نعْمِل مِنّو مطْرح يِجْمع النّاس مِتِل ما كان قبِل. بسّ مِش بسّ عَيْلِتْنا... كِلّ النّاس يَلّي عِنْدُن حنين لهيْديك الإيّام."

"قصْدِك بيْت ضْيافِة؟" سأل زِياد، وصَوْتو تْغيّر. "بسّ... بِطريقة مِخْتِلْفِة؟"

"أيْ. مِش فِنْدُق عادي. مكان بْيِحْكي قِصّة. قِصِّتْنا وقِصص كِلّ العِيَل يَلّي مِتِلْنا."

وِسام قعد على الدّرج العتيق. "بْتعِرْفوا شو أصْعب شي بِمَوْضوع الهِجْرة؟ مِش البُعْد. الخوْف مِن النِّسْيان. خَوْفْنا نِحْنا يَلّي عايْشين هوْن نِنْسى، وخَوْفْكُن إنْتو تِنْسوا."

"صحّ." همسِت يُمْنى. "أنا صار عِنْدي وْلاد، وما بعْرِف كيف بدّي خلِّيُن يْحِسّوا إنّو هَيْدا تْراثُن، إنّو هَيْدي جْذورُن."

"طيِّب،" تْدخّل زِياد. "بسّ كيف مِنْخلّي المشْروع يِمْشي؟ يَعْني عملِيّاً..."

"كِلّ واحد فينا عِنْدو شي يْقدِّمو،" قالِت يُمْنى. "إنْتَ عِنْدك خِبْرة بِإدارةْ الفنادِق. أنا بِشْتِغِل بِالتّسْويق الرّقْمي. ووِسام مْهنْدِس مِعْماري."

"I mean... maybe there's a middle ground. Not selling it, and not letting it fall apart. Bringing it back to life."

Wissam turned the camera to a page from Sitt Nada's diary. "Our house has become a station. Every summer my children return from abroad, bringing new stories with them. And everything they tell becomes part of the house's walls."

"I have an idea," said Yumna. Her eyes were shining despite her fatigue. "Let's make it a place that brings people together like it used to. But not just our family... all the people who yearn for those days."

"You mean a guesthouse?" asked Ziad, his voice changing. "But... in a different way?"

"Yes. Not just a regular hotel. A place that tells a story. Our story and the stories of all families like us."

Wissam sat on the old stairs. "You know what's the hardest thing about emigration? It's not the distance. It's the fear of forgetting. Our fear here of forgetting, and your fear there of forgetting."

"True," whispered Yumna. "I have children now, and I don't know how to make them feel that this is their heritage, these are their roots."

"Okay," Ziad interjected. "But how do we make the project work? I mean practically..."

"Each of us has something to offer," said Yumna. "You have hotel management experience. I work in digital marketing. And Wissam is an architect."

"وكمان شي،" زاد وِسام. "لْقيت بِالْعِلّية صنْدوق مِلْيان وصْفات سِتّ ندى. المْربّيات، المونة، كِلّ شي مكْتوب بِخطّ إيدا."

عْيون يُمْنى لمعِت. "مْنعْمُل مطْبخ صْغير. الضّْيوف بْيِقْدروا يِتْعلّموا كيف يِطِبْخوا أكِل تِقْليدي..."

"ومِنْحُطّ بِكِلّ غِرْفِة قِصّة،" كمّل زِياد. "قِصّة مِن يَوْمِيّات سِتّ ندى، صُوَر قديمِة..."

"وبِالْحديقة،" قال وِسام، "في مساحة كْبيرِة تحِت شجْرِةْ التّين. مْنعْمُل جلْسِة صْغيرِة، محلّ لْلقهْوِة الصُّبْح..."

سكتوا تْلاتِتْن. كِلّ واحد عم يِتْخيّل المشْروع بِطريقة مِخْتِلْفِة، بسّ كِلّْن عم يْشوفوا نفْس الحِلِم.

"سِتّ ندى كانِت دايْماً تْقول شي،" تْذكّرِت يُمْنى. "كانِت تْقول: 'البيْت يَلّي بْيِسْكُت، بيموت.' خلّينا ما نْخلّي بَيّتا يِسْكُت."

مرِّت سِتِّةْ شْهُر. البيْت صار غيْر. مِش لِأنّو تْغيّر كْتير، بسّ لِأنّو صار في حَياةْ مِن جْديد.

كِلّ صُبْح، الضّْيوف بيفيقوا على ريحِةْ القهْوِة وخِبِز الصّاج. وكِلّ ليْلِة، بْيِقْعدوا بِالجْنَيْنِة يِسْمعوا خبْرِيّات بعْض. ناس مِن كِلّ العالم، كِلّ واحد عِنْدو قُصِّةْ حنين مِخْتِلْفِة.

وعلى باب كِلّ غِرْفِة، في صفْحة مِن دفْتر سِتّ ندى، مع صورة قديمِة، وجِمْلِة كتبِتا يُمْنى: "هوْن، كِلّ ذِكرى إلا بيْت."

يوْم الجُمْعة، بِآخِر إجْتِماع زوم، سأل زِياد: "حدا فيكُن بْيِتْذكّر ليْش كِنّا بدّْنا نْبيع البيْت؟"

"And something else," added Wissam. "I found a box full of Sitt Nada's recipes in the attic. Jams, preserves, everything written in her handwriting."

Yumna's eyes lit up. "We'll make a small kitchen. Guests can learn how to cook traditional food..."

"And we'll put a story in each room," continued Ziad. "A story from Sitt Nada's diary, old photos..."

"And in the garden," said Wissam, "there's a large space under the fig tree. We'll make a small seating area, a place for morning coffee..."

All three fell silent. Each one imagining the project differently, but all seeing the same dream.

"Sitt Nada always used to say something," Yumna remembered. "She would say: 'A house that falls silent, dies.' Let's not let her house fall silent."

Six months passed. The house was different. Not because it changed much, but because it had life in it again.

Every morning, guests wake up to the smell of coffee and saj bread. And every evening, they sit in the garden listening to each other's stories. People from all over the world, each with a different story of longing.

And on each room's door, there's a page from Sitt Nada's diary, with an old photo, and a line written by Yumna. "Here, every memory has a home."

On Friday, at their last Zoom meeting, Ziad asked, "Does anyone remember why we wanted to sell the house?"

ضِحْكِت يُمْنى. "غريبة! أنا نْسيت! بسّ بْتعْرِف شو ما نْسيت؟ نْسيت إنّي بْعيدِة. صِرت حِسّ إنّي مَوْجودِة بِبيْت سِتّي كِلّ يوْم."

"يِمْكِن هَيْدا سِرّ البْيوت العتيقة،" قال وِسام وهُوِّ عم يْطفّي ضوّ البالْكوْن. "ما بْتِسْكُن فِيا بسّ هِيِّ بْتِسْكُن فيك."

Yumna laughed. "Strange! I forgot! But you know what I haven't forgotten? I forgot that I'm far away. I feel like I'm in my grandmother's house every day."

"Maybe that's the secret of old houses," said Wissam as he turned off the balcony light. "You don't just live in them. They live in you."

لِغِز الأرْزِة

The Cedar Mystery

Deep in the مِحْمية *miħmíyyi* (nature reserve) of Lebanon's cedar forests, where some أرِز *ʔáriz* (cedars) have stood for centuries watching over the mountains, something is amiss. When a former مْحقِّق *mħáʔʔiʔ* (investigator) turned village retiree receives an urgent call from the forest حارِس *ħēris* (guard), he finds himself drawn into a mystery that threatens Lebanon's natural heritage. In a place where every شجْرة *šájra* (tree) represents a piece of history, where the ضباب *ḍabāb* (fog) conceals both beauty and danger, can an experienced detective and a passionate young ranger work with the أهْل الضَّيْعة *ʔahl iḍḍáy3a* (village community) to protect these treasured trees? As they follow cryptic clues and suspicious tracks in the تْراب *trāb* (soil), they discover that the true value of the غابِة *ɣēbi* (forest) lies not just in its خشب *xášab* (wood), but in the bonds it creates between those who protect it.

Key Vocabulary

- آثار (*ʔasār*) – traces, tracks
- أرِز (*ʔáriz*) – cedar (Lebanon's national tree)
- تِحْقيق (*tiħʔīʔ*) – investigation
- تلِج (*tálij*) – snow
- جريمِة (*jarīmi*) – crime
- حرامية (*ħarāmíyyi*) – thieves
- سارِق (*sēriʔ'*) – thief
- سُوّاح (*suwwēħ*) – tourists
- سوق سَوْدا (*sūʔ sáwda*) – black market
- شُرْطة (*šúrṭa*) – police
- ضَيْعة (*ḍáy3a*) – village
- عِصابِة (*3iṣābi*)– gang
- عمّو (*3ámmu*) – uncle (respectful way to address an older man)
- كمْيوْن (*kamyōn*) – truck
- مِجْرِم (*míjrim*) – criminal
- مِخْتار (*mixtār*) – village mayor/chief
- مِنْشار (*minšār*) – saw

The Cedar Mystery	*líɣiz ilʔárzi*	لِغِز الأَرْزِة
Jawad is an old man. He used to work with the police, and now lives in a village near the cedar forest.	*jawād zálami kbīr. kēn yištíɣil ma3 iššúrṭa, u hállaʔ 3āyiš bi-ḍáy3a ʔarībi min ɣābit ilʔáriz.*	جَواد زلمي كْبير. كان يِشْتِغِل مع الشُّرْطة، وهلّأ عايِش بِضَيْعة قريبِة مِن غابِةْ الأرِز.
On Friday, Rami the forest guard called him, "Come quickly!"	*yōm iljúm3a, rāmi ḥāris ilɣābi -ttáṣal fī: "tá3a b-sír3a!"*	يوْم الجُمْعة، رامي حارِس الغابِة اتّصل فيه: "تعا بْسِرْعة!"
Jawad went to the forest. He saw a big cedar tree cut down. Rami said, "This is the third tree this month. Someone is stealing trees at night."	*jawād rāḥ 3a -lɣābi. šēf šájrit ʔáriz kbīri maʔṭū3a. rāmi ʔāl: "hay tēlit šájra ha-ššáhar. ḥáda 3am yísruʔ iššájar bi-llēl."*	جَواد راح عَ الغابِة. شاف شجْرِةْ أرِز كْبيرِة مقْطوعة. رامي قال: "هاي تالِت شجْرة هالِشّهر. حدا عم يِسْرُق الشّجر بِاللّيْل."

Jawad found a piece of paper on the ground. The paper helped him know who the thief was.	*jawād láʔa wárʔa 3ála -lʔáriḍ. -lwárʔa sē3adítu yá3rif mīn issēriʔ.*	جَواد لقى وَرْقة على الأرِض. الوَرْقة ساعدِتو يَعْرِف مين السّارِق.
He called his friends from the village. They all helped guard the forest.	*-ttáṣal bi-rifʔātu min iḍḍáy3a. kíllun sē3adu yiħírsu -lɣābi.*	اتّصل بِرِفْقاتو مِن الضَّيْعة. كِلُّن ساعدوا يِحِرْسوا الغابِة.
At night, they caught the thieves. The police came and arrested them.	*bi-llēl, másaku -lħarāmíyyi. -ššúrṭa ʔíjit u ħabasítun.*	بِاللّيْل، مسكوا الحرامية. الشُّرْطة إجِت وحبسِتُن.
Now, the forest is protected, and people from the village help guard it.	*hállaʔ, -lɣābi maħmíyyi, w-innēs min iḍḍáy3a bisē3du yiħirsū.*	هلّأ، الغابِة محْمية، والنّاس مِن الضّيْعة بيساعْدوا يِحِرْسوه.

The Cedar Mystery

لِغز الأرْزِة

Jawad Ghonem was a police investigator for thirty years. Today, after retirement, he lives in a small village near the cedar forest in Bsharri.	جَواد غنيم كان ضابِط تِحْقيق بالشُّرْطة لمِدّةْ تْلاتين سِنِة. اليوْم، بعِد التّقاعُد، بيعيش بِضَيْعة صْغيرِة قريبِة مِن غابِةْ الأرز بِبْشرّي.
Friday morning, his phone rang. It was Rami, the young forest guard. His voice was troubled. “Uncle Jawad, something’s wrong in the forest. You need to come see.”	صباح يوْم الجُمْعة، دقّ تِلِفوْنو. كان رامي، حارِس الغابِة الشّبّ. صَوْتو كان مِرْتِبِك: ”عمّو جَواد، فيّ شي غلط بِالْغابِة. لازِم تِجي تْشوف.“
Jawad put on his coat and went to the forest. The weather was cold and the fog was thick. Rami was waiting for him at the entrance to the reserve.	جَواد لِبِس كبّوتو وراح عَ الغابِة. كان الجّوْ بارِد والضّباب كْتير. رامي كان عم يْنْطُر على مدْخل المحْمية.
“What happened?” asked Jawad.	”شو صار؟“ سأل جَواد.
“Come see.” Rami walked him to an ancient cedar tree. The tree was cut down, and around it were truck tracks.	”تعا شوف.“ رامي مِشي فِي لعِنْد شجْرِةْ أرز قديمِة. الشّجْرة كانِت مقْطوعة، وحَوْلا آثار كمْيوْن.

“This is the third tree this month,” said Rami. “Someone is cutting trees at night.”	“هاي تالِت شجْرة هالشّهِر،” قال رامي. “حدا عم يِقْطع الأشْجار بِاللّيْل.”
“What did the police say?”	“شو قالِت الشُّرْطة؟”
“No one believes me. They say maybe it’s the wind.”	“ما حدا عم يْصدِّقْني. بيقولوا يِمْكِن الرّيح.”
Jawad bent down and examined the ground. He found a small piece of metal and a paper with a phone number written on it.	جَواد وَطّى وفحص الأرِض. لاقى قُطْعةْ معْدن صْغيرِة ووَرْقة مكْتوب عْلَيا رقِم تِلِفوْن.
“Rami, some people are taking advantage of the fog and cold. But they forgot that trees leave traces, and so do criminals.”	“رامي، في ناس عم تِسْتفيد مِن الضّباب والبرِد. بسّ نِسْيوا إنّو الأشْجار بْتِتْرُك آثار، والمِجرْمين كمان.”

لِغز الأرْزِة

The Cedar Mystery

الضّباب كان عم يْلِفّ غابِةْ الأرز بِبْشرّي مِتِل كِلّ صُبْحِيّات الشِّتي. جَواد غنيم ، الِمْحقِّق المِتْقاعِد، كان قاعِد بِبَيْتو الِصّْغير بِالضّيْعة، عم يِشْرب قهِوْتو ويِتْطلّع على الجْبال البيْضا مِن الشِّباك.

The fog was wrapping around the cedar forest in Bsharri like every winter morning. Jawad Ghonem, the retired investigator, was sitting in his small village house, drinking his coffee and looking at the white mountains through the window.

بعِد تْلاتين سِنِة بِالشُّرْطة بِالْمدينِة، قرّر يْعيش بِهالضّيْعة الهادْيِة. "بدّي إرْتاح مِن المشاكِل والجرايِم ،" هيْك قال لمرْتو. بسّ شكْلو إنّو المشاكِل لاحْقِتو للْجبل.

After thirty years with the police in the city, he decided to live in this quiet village. "I want to rest from problems and crimes," that's what he told his wife. But it seems the problems followed him to the mountain.

دقّ تِلِفوْنو. كان رامي، حارِس المحْمية الشّبّ يَلّي بيحِبّ الأرز مِتِل ما بيحِبّ أهْلو.

His phone rang. It was Rami, the young reserve guard who loves the cedars as much as he loves his family.

"عمّو جَواد، لازِم تِجي بْسِرْعة. في كارْثِة بِالْغابِة!"

"Uncle Jawad, you need to come quickly. There's a disaster in the forest!"

جَواد لِبِس كبّوتو التِّقيل وطُلِع. كان الجّوّ بارِد كْتير، والتّلْج عم يْغطّي الطّريق. لمّا وُصِل عَ المحْمية، لاقى رامي عم يِنْطْرو عَ المدْخل، وِجّو أصْفر.

Jawad put on his heavy coat and went out. The weather was very cold, and snow was covering the road. When he reached the reserve, he found Rami waiting for him at the entrance, his face pale.

"تعا شوف شو عِمْلوا!" مِشي رامي بْسِرْعة وجَواد لِحْقو. وُصْلوا لمنْطقة بْعيدِة شْوَيّ بِالْغابِة. هوْنيك شافوا المنْظر الحزين: شجْرِة أرز عُمْرا مِئات السِّنين مقْطوعة مِن جِذْعا.

"Come see what they did!" Rami walked quickly and Jawad followed him. They reached a somewhat remote area in the forest. There they saw the sad sight: a cedar tree hundreds of years old, cut from its trunk.

"هاي تالِت وِحْدِة هالشّهر،" قال رامي بِحِزن. "عم يِجوا بِاللّيْل. بْيِقْطعوا الشّجْرة وبْياخْدُوَا بِكامْيوْن صْغير. خشب الأرِز غالي كْتير بِالسّوق السَّوْدا."

"This is the third one this month," Rami said sadly. "They come at night. They cut the tree and take it in a small truck. Cedar wood is very expensive on the black market."

جَواد وَطّى وفحص محلّ القطِع. كان نْضيف ومِسْتْوي. "هَيْدا شِغِل مِحْتِرِف. عِنْدُن معدّات خاصّة."

Jawad bent down and examined the cut site. It was clean and even. "This is professional work. They have special equipment."

"خبّرْت الشُّرْطة،" قال رامي. "بسّ قالولي ما في أدلِّة. يِمْكِن الرّيح، يِمْكِن التّلِج... بسّ أنا بعْرِف الغابِة. هَيْدا شِغِل عِصابِة."

“I told the police,” said Rami. “But they said there’s no evidence. Maybe it’s the wind, maybe the snow... but I know the forest. This is the work of a gang.”

جَواد مِشي حَوْل المحلّ. عْيونو المْدرّبِة مِن سْنين التِّحْقيق لقطِت شي على الأرض: قِطْعِةْ معْدن صْغيرِة مِن مِنْشار، ووَرْقة مِطْوية فِيا رِقم تِلِفوْن.

Jawad walked around the area. His eyes, trained from years of investigation, caught something on the ground: a small piece of metal from a saw, and a folded paper with a phone number.

“شو هَيْدا؟” سأل رامي.

“What’s this?” asked Rami.

“أوّل خيْط بِالتِّحْقيق. بسّ خلّينا ما نِسْتعْجِل. العِصابات المْنظّمِة خِطْرة، وهَيْدي مِش عِصابِة صْغيرِة. حدا عم يِدْفعْلُن مصاري كْتير مشان يْخاطْروا هيْك.”

“The first thread in the investigation. But let’s not rush. Organized gangs are dangerous, and this isn’t a small gang. Someone is paying them a lot of money to take such risks.”

رِجْعوا عَ المكْتب الِصّْغير بِمدْخل المحْمية. رامي صبّ شاي سُخِن وقعدوا يْفكْروا.

They returned to the small office at the reserve entrance. Rami poured hot tea and they sat thinking.

“المِشْكْلِة أكْبر مِن شجْرة مقْطوعة،” قال جَواد. “الأرز رمز وَطني. كِلّ شجْرة عُمْرا مِيّات السِّنين بْتِسْوى تاريخ.”

“The problem is bigger than a cut tree,” said Jawad. “The cedar is a national symbol. Each tree hundreds of years old is worth a history.”

"كِلّ الحِرّاس بِالْمنْطقة لازِم يْعِرْفوا شو عم يْصير،" قال رامي. "رح إتِّصِل فِيُن."

"All the guards in the area need to know what's happening," said Rami. "I'll call them."

"ما تْخبِّر حدا بعِد،" قاطعو جَواد. "ما مْنعْرِف مين مِتْورّط. الخشب الغالي بيغيِّر النّاس."

"Don't tell anyone yet," Jawad interrupted. "We don't know who's involved. Expensive wood changes people."

بِنفْس الوَقِت، سِمْعوا صوْت سِيّارة عم تْقرِّب. جَواد طِلِع مِن المكْتب وشاف باص سُوّاح عم يوقف عَ المدْخل.

At that moment, they heard a vehicle approaching. Jawad stepped out of the office and saw a tourist bus stopping at the entrance.

"هَيْدا غريب،" قال رامي. "ما في رِحْلات سِياحية بكّير هيْك."

"This is strange," said Rami. "There are no tourist trips this early."

نِزِل مِن الباص خمْس رْجال. كانوا لابْسين تْياب سُوّاح، بسّ جَواد لاحظ إنّو حركِتْن ما كانِت طبيعية. "شكْلُن سُوّاح مْزيّفين،" همس لرامي.

Five men got off the bus. They were wearing tourist clothes, but Jawad noticed their movements weren't natural. "They look like fake tourists," he whispered to Rami.

"صباح الخيْر!" قال كْبيرُن. "نِحْنا مجْموعة مِن الأجانِب، بدّْنا نْزور الغابِة."

"Good morning!" said the oldest one. "We're a group of foreigners, we want to visit the forest."

"بِعْتِذِر، المحْمية مْسكّرة اليوْم،" جاوَب جَواد بْسِرْعة. "في صِيانة."

"Sorry, the reserve is closed today," Jawad replied quickly. "There's maintenance."

الرْجال تْطلّعوا بِبعْضُن. "بسّ نِحْنا جايّين مِن بْعيد..."

The men looked at each other. "But we've come from far away..."

"تعوا بُكْرا. اليوْم مُسْتحيل."

"Come tomorrow. Today is impossible."

رِجْعوا عَ الباص ومِشْيوا. جَواد كتب رقِم لَوْحِةْ السِّيّارة.

They returned to the bus and left. Jawad wrote down the license plate number.

"ليْش كذّبِت عْلَيْن؟" سأل رامي.

"Why did you lie to them?" asked Rami.

"شِفِت إيدِيْن؟ خِشْنِة وفِيا جْروح. هَيْدوْل مِش سُوّاح. عِمّال بْيِشْتِغْلوا بِالْخشب."

"Did you see their hands? Rough and scarred. These aren't tourists. They're wood workers."

بعِد ساعة، اتّصل جَواد بِرْفيقو القديم بِالشُّرْطة. "مْحمّد، بدّي معْلومات عن رقِم سِيّارة... وكمان عن رقِم تِلِفوْن."

An hour later, Jawad called his old friend in the police. "Mohammed, I need information about a car number... and also a phone number."

بِاللّيْل، رِجِع جَواد عَ البيت وقعد يْفكِّر. خِبْرْتو قالِتْلو إنّو في شي أكْبر مِن سِرْقِةْ خشب. في حدا كْبير وَرا المَوْضوع.

In the evening, Jawad returned home and sat thinking. His experience told him this was bigger than wood theft. Someone powerful was behind it.

تاني يوْم، إجا الجَواب مِن رْفيقو. الباص مْسجّل بِإسِم شِرْكِة سِياحية وَهْمية، والتِّلِفوْن بِإسِم تاجِر خشب معْروف بِطْرابْلُس.

The next day, the answer came from his friend. The bus was registered to a fake tourism company, and the phone belonged to a well-known wood merchant in Tripoli.

"هلّأ عْرِفْنا مين وَرا المَوْضوع،" قال جَواد لرامي. "بسّ المْهِمّ نعْرِف كيف مِنْوقِّفُن قبِل ما يِرْجعوا."

"Now we know who's behind this," Jawad told Rami. "But the important thing is knowing how to stop them before they return."

"شو مْنعْمُل؟"

"How will we do it?"

"عِنْدي فِكْرة... بسّ رح نِحْتاج مُساعدِة مِن أهْل الضّيْعة."

"I have an idea... but we'll need help from the villagers."

لِغز الأرْزة

كان الضّباب كْتير على جْبال بْشرّي، حتّى إنّو ما بِتْشوف أبْعد مِن خمْس مْتار قِدّامك. جَواد غنيم وِقِف على شِبّاك بيْتو الحجر القديم، عَيْنو على الغابِة يَلّي بْتِبْعُد نُصّ ساعة مشي. أرْبْعين سِنِة مِن حَياتو قضّاها بيلاحِق المِجرْمين بِبَيْروت، وفكّر إنّو هوْن، بيْن الأرِز العتيق والتّلْج الأبْيَض، رح يْلاقي السّلام يَلّي دايْماً حِلِم فيه.

"شجْرِةْ الأرِز بْتاخُد مِيةْ سِنِة لتِكْبر، وخمْس دْقايِق لتِنْقطع،" هالجِّمْلِة قالا مرّة رامي حارِس المحْمية. جَواد ما كان يَعْرِف إنّو هالْكلام رح يِرْجع يْدِقّ بِراسو هالصُّبِح.

السّاعة كانِت بعْدا سبْعة الصُّبُح لمّا دقّ تِلِفوْنو. صوْت رامي كان عم يِرْجُف: "عمّو جَواد... المْصيبِة صارِت. رح تِفْهم كِلّ شي لمّا تِجي."

لِبِس كبّوتو الشّتَوي وطِلِع. هُوّي يَلّي عُمْرو ما خاف مِن مِجْرِم وَلا مِن رْصاصة، حسّ بِقشْعريرة وهُوّي عم يِمْشي بيْن شجر الأرِز. كِلّ شجْرة مِتِل عمود مِن أعْمِدِةْ التّاريخ، شاهدِة على آلاف السّْنين.

رامي كان واقِف حدّ كامْيون الدّفْع الرُّباعي تبع المحْمية. "تعا شوف،" قال وهُوِّ عم يْأشِّر على التُّراب المْغطّى بِالتّلِج. آثار كامْيون كْبير، وقُطع خشب مْتِناثْرة، وشي أسْوَد على التّلْج الأبْيَض.

"زيْت؟" سأل جَواد.

"مِن المكنة يَلّي سْتعْملوا. هاي المرّة ما سْتعْملوا مِنْشار عادي. جابوا مكنات جْديدِة، سريعة وبلا صوْت. عم يِتْعلّموا مِن أخْطاءُن."

The Cedar Mystery

The fog was so thick over the Bsharri mountains that you couldn't see more than five meters ahead. Jawad Ghonem stood at the window of his old stone house, his eyes on the forest half an hour's walk away. He had spent forty years of his life chasing criminals in Beirut, thinking that here, among the ancient cedars and white snow, he would find the peace he had always dreamed of.

"A cedar tree takes a hundred years to grow, and five minutes to cut down," Rami, the reserve guard, had once said. Jawad didn't know these words would echo in his head this morning.

It was still seven in the morning when his phone rang. Rami's voice was trembling. "Uncle Jawad... disaster has struck. You'll understand everything when you come."

He put on his winter coat and went out. He who had never feared criminal or bullet felt a shiver as he walked among the cedar trees. Each tree was like a pillar of history, witness to thousands of years.

Rami was standing next to the reserve's four-wheel-drive vehicle. "Come see," he said, pointing to the snow-covered ground. Tracks from a large truck, scattered wood pieces, and something black on the white snow.

"Oil?" asked Jawad.

"From the machine they used. This time they didn't use a regular saw. They brought modern equipment, fast and quiet. They're learning from their mistakes."

وْصلوا لموْقع الجريمِة. شجْرةْ أرز ضخْمِة، عُمْرا يِمْكِن خْمِسْمِيِّةْ سِنِة، مقْطوعة مِن جِذْعا بِشكِل مِحْتِرِف. جَواد وَطّى وفحص محلّ القطِع.

"شوف كيف نْضيف القصّ،" قال. "هَيْدا شِغِل مِحْتِرِف. في خِبْرة هوْن."

"يا ريْت بسّ هيْك،" قال رامي. "تعا معي."

مِشيوا شْوَيّ لقِدّام. كان في شجِرْتيْن تانْيين مقْطوعين بِنفْس الطّريقة. التّْلاتِة مِخْتارين بِعِنايِة: شجر قديم، بْعاد عن الطّريق الرّئيسي، ومْخبّايّين وَرا شجر تاني.

"هَيْدي تالِت ليْلِة مْنِسْمع صوْت شاحْنات،" قال رامي. "بسّ المِشْكْلِة إنّو في حِراسِة على كِلّ المداخِل. كيف عم يْفوتوا؟"

جَواد مِشي حوْل المحلّ. أرْبعين سِنِة بِالتّحْقيق علّمِتوا إنّو الجريمِة مِتِل الخيْط: إذا مسك طرفو، بيكِرّ كِلّو.

حرّك التّْراب بِحذر بِطرف صِبّاطو. "المِشْكْلِة مِش كيف عم يْفوتوا. المِشْكْلِة مين عم يْسهِلّن الفَوْتِة." رفع قِطْعةْ معْدن صْغيرِة مِن الأرِض. "هَيْدي مِن مِنْشار كهْربا مِتْطوِّر. مِش مِن النّوْع يَلّي بْتْلاقي بِأيّ محلّ. وهَيْدي..." وَطّى ولقط وَرْقة صْغيرِة، "فاتورة مِن محطّةْ بِنْزين على طريق طْرابْلُس."

رامي هزّ راسو: "بْتعْرِف شو أصْعب شي بِالْمَوْضوع؟ إنّو هالشّجر صاروا جِزِء مِنّي. كِلّ وِحْدِة بعْرف شكْلا، وعُمْرا، وأيْمتى بْتِزْهِر. كِلّ ما بْشوف وِحْدِة مقْطوعة، بْحِسّ حدا نْقتل مِن عيْلْتي."

جَواد تْأمّل بِالْمطْرح. "في شي غلط بِالصّورة. العِصابات ما بْتْخاطِر هيْك إلّا إذا في حدا كْبير وَراها. خشب الأرِز غالي، صحّ، بسّ المُخاطرة أغْلى."

They reached the crime scene. A huge cedar tree, perhaps five hundred years old, professionally cut from its trunk. Jawad bent down and examined the cut site.

“See how clean the cut is,” he said. “This is professional work. There’s expertise here.”

“If only that were all,” said Rami. “Come with me.”

They walked a bit further. There were two more trees cut in the same way. All three were carefully chosen: old trees, far from the main road, and hidden behind other trees.

“This is the third night we’ve heard trucks,” said Rami. “But the problem is there’s security at all entrances. How are they getting in?”

Jawad walked around the area. Forty years of investigation had taught him that crime is like a thread: if you grab one end, you’ll find the whole ball.

He carefully moved the soil with the tip of his shoe. “The problem isn’t how they’re getting in. The problem is who’s making it easy for them to get in.” He picked up a small piece of metal from the ground. “This is from an advanced electric saw. Not the kind you’d find in any shop. And this...” he bent down and picked up a small piece of paper, “is a receipt from a gas station on the Tripoli road.”

Rami shook his head. “You know what’s hardest about this? These trees have become part of me. I know each one’s shape, age, and when it blooms. Every time I see one cut down, I feel like someone from my family has been killed.”

Jawad contemplated the scene. “Something’s wrong with this picture. Gangs don’t take risks like this unless someone powerful is behind them. Cedar wood is expensive, yes, but the risk is more expensive.”

رِجْعوا عَ المكْتب الِصّغير. رامي صبّ قهْوِة وقعد يِشْرح: "مِن سِنِة، صار في مشْروع سِياحي كْبير عم يِنْبنى بِالْمنْطقة. فيلل فخْمِة كِلّا مِن الخشب. المِسْتثْمِر عم بيقول إنّو بْيِسْتَوْرِد الخشب مِن برّا، بسّ ما حدا شاف وْراق إسْتيراد."

"مين هالْمِسْتثْمِر؟"

"رجُل أعْمال كْبير، عِنْدو علاقات قَوية. إسْمو..."

قاطعو صوْت سِيّارة عم تْقرِّب. باص سِياحي وِقِف عَ مدْخل المحْمية. نِزِل مِنّو خمْس رْجال بِتْياب سُوّاح، بسّ حركِتُن كانِت بْتوحي بِشي تاني.

"صباح الخيْر!" قال كْبيرُن. "نِحْنا مجْموعِةْ سُوّاح، جايِّين نْزور المحْمية."

جَواد دقّق بِوْجوهُن. عْيون مِتْوَتِّرة، إيديْن خِشْنين، وحركات مِش طبيعية. "مْنِعْتِذِر، المحْمية مْسكِّرة اليوْم للصِّيانِة."

"بسّ نِحْنا جايِّين مِن بْعيد..."

"بُكْرا أحْسن. اليوْم في فريق صِيانِة عم يِشْتِغِل بِالْغابِة."

تْبادلوا نظرات مِتْوَتِّرة ورِجْعوا عَ الباص. جَواد كتب رقِم السِّيّارة.

"شو هالْمسْرحية؟" سأل رامي.

"هَيْدوْل مِش سُوّاح. جايِّين يِسْتكِشْفوا المطْرح. شِفِت كيف كانوا عم يِدِرْسوا المداخِل والطِّرْقات؟"

They returned to the small office. Rami poured coffee and started explaining. “A year ago, they started a big tourism project in the area. Luxury villas, all made of wood. The investor claims he imports the wood from abroad, but no one has seen any import papers.”

“Who’s this investor?”

“A big businessman with strong connections. His name...”

He was interrupted by the sound of an approaching vehicle. A tourist bus stopped at the reserve entrance. Five men in tourist clothes got out, but their movements suggested something else.

“Good morning!” called the oldest one. “We’re a group of tourists, here to visit the reserve.”

Jawad studied their faces. Nervous eyes, rough hands, and unnatural movements. “Sorry, the reserve is closed today for maintenance.”

“But we’ve come from far away...”

“Tomorrow would be better. Today there’s a maintenance team working in the forest.”

They exchanged worried looks and returned to the bus. Jawad wrote down the car number.

“What was that performance about?” asked Rami.

“Those weren’t tourists. They came to scout the location. Did you see how they were studying the entrances and roads?”

اتّصل جَواد بِرْفيقو القديم بِقْوى الأمِن، طلب مِنّو يِكْشُف على رقِم السِّيّارة. وبِنْفس الوَقِت، طلب مِن رامي يْجمِّع معْلومات عن المشْروع السِّياحي وصاحْبو.

"المِشْكْلِة إنّو كِلّ ما قطعوا شجْرة، بيموت جزِء مِن تاريخْنا،" قال رامي. "هَيْدي الشّجر شافِت الفينيقِيّين والرّومان والعِثْمانيين... وهلّأ عم تْموت بِقصِّةْ مِنْشار."

"ما تْخاف،" قال جَواد. "في ناس بِتْفكِّر إنّو المصاري أهمّ مِن التّاريخ. بسّ نِحْنا مْنعْرِف إنّو في إشْيا ما بْتِنْشرى: الضّمير وحُبّ الأرِض."

بعِد يوْميْن، وُصْلِت المعْلومات مِن كِلّ الجِهّات. الباص مْسجّل بإسْم شِرْكِة سِياحية وَهْمية، والمشْروع السِّياحي تابِع لشِرْكِةْ "الجبل الأخْضر" يَلّي بْيِمْلِكا رجُل الأعْمال وسيم الدُّويْهي.

"عِنْدي خِطة،" قال جَواد لرامي. "بسّ بدّْنا مُساعدِة مِن أهْل الضّيْعة."

بِاللّيْل، جْتمعوا بِمْضيافِةْ الشّيْخ سْليْمان، مِخْتار الضّيْعة. كان في عِشْرين رِجّال مِن العِيَل الكْبيرِة بِالضّيْعة.

"الأرز مِش بسّ شجر،" قال المِخْتار. "هُوّي هَوِيِّتْنا. يَلّي بْيِقْطع شجْرةْ أرز، كإنّو عم يِقْطع جْذورْنا."

الكِلّ وافق يْساعِد. قسّموا الغابِة لمناطِق، وكِلّ مجْموعة صارِتْ مسْؤولة عن منْطقة. حطّوا كاميرات صْغيرِة مِخْفِيّة، وجهّزوا نِظام إنْذار بسيط: صفير طَويل مِن الصّوفيْرة إذا في شي مشْبوه.

Jawad called his old friend in security forces, asking him to check the vehicle number. At the same time, he asked Rami to gather information about the tourism project and its owner.

“The problem is that every time they cut a tree, a part of our history dies,” said Rami. “These trees saw the Phoenicians, Romans, and Ottomans... and now they’re dying with the stroke of a saw.”

“Don’t worry,” said Jawad. “Some people think money is more important than history. But we know there are things that can’t be bought: conscience and love of the land.”

Two days later, information came in from all sides. The bus was registered to a fake tourism company, and the tourism project belonged to “Green Mountain Company,” owned by businessman Wassim Al-Doueihy.

“I have a plan,” Jawad told Rami. “But we need help from the villagers.”

At night, they gathered in Sheikh Suleiman’s guest house, the village mayor. Twenty men from the village’s prominent families were present.

“The cedar isn’t just a tree,” said the mayor. “It’s our identity. Whoever cuts a cedar tree is cutting our roots.”

Everyone agreed to help. They divided the forest into zones, with each group responsible for an area. They placed hidden small cameras and prepared a simple warning system: a long horn blast if anything suspicious was spotted.

مرِّت تْلات لَيالي والكِلّ عم يْراقِب. بِليْلِةْ الجُمْعة، وَقِت نُص اللّيْل، طِلِع صوْت الصّوفيْرة. جَواد ورامي وشباب الضّيْعة تْحرّكوا بْسِرْعة، وُصْلوا عَ المطْرح وشافوا كمْيوْن كْبير وتْلات رْجال عم يْجهْزوا المْناشير.

"وَقْفوا!" صرخ جَواد، وطِلْعِت الأضْوية مِن كِلّ الجِهّات. رْجال الضّيْعة طوّقوا المطْرح.

العِمّال حاولوا يِهرْبوا، بسّ ما كان في مجال. الشُّرْطة وُصْلِت بعِد نُصّ ساعة. بِالتِّحْقيق، العِمّال عْترفوا إنّو في حدا كْبير وَراهُن، بسّ ما حِكْيوا مين.

جَواد ما نطر. راح عِنْد رْفيقو الصّحافي بِبَيْروت. بعِد أُسْبوع، طِلِع تِحْقيق كْبير بِالْجريدة عن تِجارِةْ خشب الأرز غيْر الشّرْعية، مع صُوَر وأدلِّة. الفضيحة كانِت كْبيرِة، والشِّرْكِة السِّياحية سكّرِت.

"بْتعْرِف شو أحْلى شي بِالْمَوْضوع؟" قال رامي لجَواد هِنّي وْقاعْدين تحِت شجْرِةْ أرز عُمْرا ألْف سِنِة. "إنّو النّاس صارِت تِفْهم قدّيْش هالْغابِة غالْيِة. هلّأ كِلّ يوْم في مِتْطَوْعين مِن الضّيْعة بْيِجوا يْساعْدوا بِالْحِراسِة."

جَواد بتسم. "المِجْرِم بيفكِّر إنّو الجريمِة سهْلِة لِأنّو الشّجْرة ما بْتِحْكي. بسّ نِسي إنّو الأرْض بْتِحْكي، والنّاس بْتِحْكي، والتّاريخ بْيِحْكي."

ومِن هَيْداك النْهار، ما حدا تْجرّأ يِقْطع شجْرة مِن المحْمية. وكِلّ ما حدا بْيِسْأل جَواد: "ليْش تركِت المدينِة وجيت عَ الجبل؟" بيجاوِب: "لِأنّو في جرايِم أكْبر مِن جرايِم المدينِة. قطِع شجْرة عُمْرا ألْف سِنِة، هَيْدي جريمة ضُدّ التّاريخ كِلّو."

Three nights passed with everyone watching. On Friday night, at midnight, the horn sounded. Jawad, Rami, and the village youth moved quickly. They reached the spot and saw a large truck and three men preparing their saws.

“Stop!” shouted Jawad, and lights came on from all directions. The village men had surrounded the area.

The workers tried to escape, but there was no way out. The police arrived half an hour later. During questioning, the workers admitted there was someone powerful behind them, but wouldn’t say who.

Jawad didn’t wait. He went to his journalist friend in Beirut. A week later, a major investigation appeared in the newspaper about illegal cedar wood trading, with photos and evidence. The scandal was huge, and the tourism company shut down.

“You know what’s the best thing about this?” Rami said to Jawad as they sat under a thousand-year-old cedar tree. “People have started to understand how precious this forest is. Now volunteers from the village come every day to help with guarding.”

Jawad smiled. “A criminal thinks the crime is easy because trees don’t talk. But he forgets that the earth talks, people talk, and history talks.”

From that day on, no one dared to cut trees from the reserve. And whenever someone asked Jawad, “Why did you leave the city and come to the mountain?” he would answer, “Because there are crimes bigger than city crimes. Cutting a thousand-year-old tree is a crime against all of history.”

مشروع الحديقة

The Garden Project

Among the most vulnerable populations in Lebanon are Syrian refugees living in informal مُخيّمات *muxayyamēt* (settlements/camps) in the البْقاع *lib?ā3* (Bekaa Valley), where summer temperatures soar and winter brings bitter برد *bárid* (cold) and وَحِل *wáħil* (mud). But even in these harsh conditions, between the خِيَم *xíyam* (tents), the human spirit finds ways to create beauty and sustenance. How can a small patch of أرِض فاضْيِة *?áriḍ fāḍya* (empty land) become a source of not just food, but أمل *?ámal* (hope) and community? This story explores how traditional agricultural knowledge, carried across borders through ذِكْرَيات *zikrayēt* (memories) and saved بِذِر *bízir* (seeds), can transform refugee life and build unexpected bridges between communities.

Key Vocabulary

- برّا (*bárra*) – abroad
- برميل (*barmīl*) – barrel
- بلدي (*báladi*) – local, traditional
- بلدية (*baladíyyi*) – municipality
- بير (*bīr*) – (water) well
- تِصْريف (*tiṣrīf*) – drainage
- تْعاوُن (*t3āwun*) – cooperation
- تقاليد (*taʔālīd*) – traditions
- جِسِر (*jísir*) – bridge
- جيران (*jīrān*) – neighbors
- خُضْرا (*xúḍra*) – vegetables
- خيْمِة (*xēmi*) – tent
- زِراعة (*zirā3a*) – farming/agriculture
- سْقايِة (*sʔēyi*) – watering
- شاويش (*šēwīš*) – settlement coordinator/leader
- صاحِب الأرِض (*ṣāħib ilʔáriḍ*) – landowner
- محاصيل (*maħāṣīl*) – crops

- مُزارِع (*muzēri3*) – farmer
- مُنظّمات إنْسانية (*munaẓẓamēt ʔinsēníyyi*) – humanitarian organizations
- مُوافقة (*muwēfaʔa*) – approval

A1

The Garden Project	***mašrū3 ilḫadīʔa***	**مشْروع الحديقة**
Noura and her family live in a settlement in the Bekaa. Noura knows a lot about farming.	*nūra u 3ēlíta 3āyšīn bi-muxáyyam bi-libʔā3. nūra btá3rif ktīr 3an izzirā3a.*	نورا وعيْلِتا عايْشين بِمُخيّم بِالِبْقاع. نورا بْتعْرِف كْتير عن الزِّراعة.
One day she saw empty land in the settlement. She said, "We can grow vegetables here!"	*fī márra šēfit ʔáriḍ fāḍyi bi-lmuxáyyam. ʔālit: "mníʔdar nízra3 xúḍra hōn!"*	في مرّة شافِت أرِض فاضْية بِالْمُخيّم. قالِت: "مْنِقْدر نِزْرع خُضْرا هوْن!"
She went to talk to Shawish Adel. He said, "Good idea."	*rāḫit tíḫki ma3 iššēwīš 3ādil. ʔāl: "fíkra ḫílwi."*	راحِت تِحْكي مع الشّاويش عادِل. قال: "فِكْرة حِلْوة."

They brought big barrels and soil. The women in the settlement worked together. Emm Omar brought seeds from Syria: tomatoes, cucumbers, and parsley.	*jēbu b-rāmīl kbīri u trāb. -nniswēn bi-lmuxáyyam t3āwánu ma3 ba3ḍ. ʔimm 3úmar jēbit bízir min sūríya: banadūra u xyār u baʔdūnis.*	جابوا بْراميل كْبيرِة وتْراب. النِّسْوان بِالْمُخيّم تْعاوَنوا مع بعْض. إمّ عُمر جابِت بِذِر مِن سورِيا: بندورة وخْيار وبقْدونِس.
Each family got two barrels for planting. The children help with watering every day.	*kill 3ēli ṣār 3índa barmīlēn la-zirā3a. -liwlēd bisē3du bi-lsaʔēyi kill yōm.*	كِلّ عيْلِة صار عِنْدا برْميلَيْن للزِّراعة. الوْلاد بيساعْدوا بِالسّقايِة كِلّ يوْم.
Now there are fresh vegetables in the settlement, and people are happy. Even Lebanese neighbors come to see the garden.	*hállaʔ fī xúḍra ṭāza bi-lmuxáyyam, u -nnēs mabsūṭīn. ɦátta -ljīrān illibnēniyyīn byiju byitfárraju 3ála -lɦadīʔa.*	هلّأ في خُضْرا طازة بِالْمُخيّم، والنّاس مْبسوطين. حتّى الجيران اللِّبْنانِيّين بْيِجوا بْيِتْفرّجوا على الحديقة.

The Garden Project

مشْروع الحديقة

Noura and her family live in a small informal settlement in the Bekaa Valley, near Zahle. The settlement has about 20 tents, with one family in each tent. In summer, the sun is very strong and the ground is dry. In winter, there's lots of mud and cold.

نورا وعيْلِتا عايْشين بِمُخيّم صْغير بِسهْل البْقاع، قريب مِن زحْلِة. المْخيّم في حَوالي ٢٠ خيْمِة، وكِلّ خيْمِة فِيا عيْلِة. بِالصّيْف، الشّمِس قَوية كْتير والأرِض ناشْفِة. وبِالشّتي، في كْتير وَحِل وبرِد.

Noura, who used to have land in rural Aleppo, saw a small empty space between the tents. She asked Shawish Adel, the settlement coordinator, "Can we grow some vegetables here?"

نورا، يَلّي كان عِنْدا أرِض بِريف حلب، شافِت قُطْعة صْغيرِة فاضْيِة بيْن الخِيَم. سألِت الشّاويش عادِل، مسْؤول المُخيّم: "فينا نِزْرع هوْن شْوَيِّة خُضْرا؟"

The Shawish said, "We need to ask the landowner and get municipal approval. But if they agree, I'm with you."

الشّاويش قال: "لازِم نِسْأل صاحِب الأرِض، ونْجيب مُوافقة مِن البلدية. بسّ إذا وافقوا، أنا معِك."

They went to the landowner, Abu Ghassan, and explained the idea. He agreed but said, “You can’t build anything permanent. And when the year ends, you must return the land as it was.”	راحوا مع صاحِب الأرِض، أبو غسّان، وشْرحولوا الفِكْرة. وافق بسّ قال: ”ما فيكُن تِبْنوا شي ثابِت. وبسّ تِخْلص السِّنِة، لازِم تْرْجْعوا الأرِض مِتِل ما كانِت.“
Noura gathered the women. Emm Omar brought seeds from Syria, and Emm Hassan had farming experience. They decided to plant in boxes and barrels, not directly in the ground. This way they could move the plants if needed.	نورا جمّعِت النِّسْوان. إمّ عُمر جابِت بِذِر مِن سورِيا، وإم حسن عِنْدا خِبْرة بِالزِّراعة. قرّروا يِزْرعوا بِصْناديق وبْراميل، مِش بِالْأرِض مْباشرة. هيْك بْيِقْدروا يِنِقْلوا الزِّراعة إذا لازِم.
They got water from the well and made a schedule: each family waters for one day. The children started helping after school. They planted lettuce, tomatoes, and parsley. Also basil, because Emm Omar said, “The smell of our homeland.”	جابوا ميّ مِن البير، وعِمْلوا جدْول: كِلّ عيْلِة بْتِسْقي يوْم. الِوْلاد صاروا يْساعْدوا بعِد المدْرِسِة. زرعوا خسّ، بندورة، وبقْدونِس. حتّى الحبق، لِأنّو إمّ عُمر قالِت: ”ريحِةْ بلدْنا.“
The project is small, but growing slowly. Now, when someone passes by the settlement, they see something green and beautiful between the tents.	المشْروع صْغير، بسّ عم بْيِكْبر شْوَيّ شْوَيّ. هلّأ، لمّا حدا بْيِمْرُق مِن عِنْد المُخيّم، بيشوف شي أخْضر وحِلو بيْن الخِيَم.

مشْروع الحديقة

The Garden Project

بِمُخيّم العَوْدِة، حدّ زحْلِة، في عِشْرين خيْمِة مْرتّبِة على شكِل مْربّع، وَسطا ساحة صْغيرِة. المُخيّم واقِف على أرْض مِسْتأجْرة مِن أبو غسّان، مْزارِع لِبْناني طيِّب، بسّ حريص على أرْضو. بِالصّيْف، بْترْتِفِع الحرارة لفوْق الأرْبْعين، وبِالشِّتي بْتِنْزل تحِت الصُّفِر، والوَحِل بيغرِّق المداخِل.

In Al-Awda settlement near Zahle, twenty tents are arranged in a square, with a small courtyard in the middle. The settlement stands on land rented from Abu Ghassan, a kind Lebanese farmer who's protective of his land. In summer, temperatures rise above forty degrees, and in winter they drop below zero, with mud flooding the entrances.

نورا، يَلّي كانِت مْهنْدْسِة زِراعية بِحلب، ما قِدْرِت تِتْحمّل تْضلّ تِتْفرّج على هالأرْض الفاضْية بيْن الخِيَم. "معْقول نِحْنا يَلّي كِنّا مْزارْعين، نِشْتْري كِلّ شي مِن السّوق؟" قالِت هالْحكي لجارِتا إمّ عُمر يَلّي كان عِنْدا بيْت وبْساتين بِالْغوطة.

Noura, who was an agricultural engineer in Aleppo, couldn't bear to keep looking at the empty space between the tents. "How is it possible that we, who were farmers, are buying everything from the market?" she said this to her neighbor Emm Omar, who used to have a house and orchard in Ghouta.

"واللّه عِنْدِك حقّ،" قالِت إمّ عُمر. "بسّ شو رح يْقول الشّاويش عادِل؟ وصاحِب الأرِض؟ والبلدية؟"

“By God, you’re right,” said Emm Omar. “But what will Shawish Adel say? And the landowner? And the municipality?”

نورا ما سْتسْلمت. راحِت عِنْد الشّاويش عادِل، يَلّي بيمثِّل المُخيّم قِدّام السُّلْطات. "عِنْدي فِكْرة،" قالِتْلو. "بدّْنا نِزْرع خِضْرا للْعِيل. ما رح نِبْني شي ثابِت، وما رح نِحْفُر الأرِض. رح نِسْتعْمِل بْراميل وصْناديق بسّ."

Noura didn’t give up. She went to Shawish Adel, who represents the settlement to authorities. “I have an idea,” she told him. “We want to grow vegetables for the families. We won’t build anything permanent, and we won’t dig up the land. We’ll just use barrels and boxes.”

الشّاويش فكّر شْوَيّ. "فِكْرة مْنيحة، بسّ في شْروط. لازم مُوافقِةْ المالِك والبلدية. ولازِم نْكون حريصين ما نْخالِف القْوانين."

The Shawish thought for a moment. “Good idea, but there are conditions. We need the owner’s and municipality’s approval. And we must be careful not to break any laws.”

المُفاوْضات مع أبو غسّان دامِت أُسْبوع. وافق بسّ حطّ شْروط: ممْنوع البِنا الثّابِت، ولازِم يِقْدْروا يْشيلوا كِلّ شي بِأيّ وَقِت، والميّ مِن البير مِش مِن شبكِةْ الميّ.

Negotiations with Abu Ghassan lasted a week. He agreed but set conditions: no permanent construction, everything must be removable at any time, and water must come from the well, not the water network.

بسّ صار في مُوافقة، جْتمعِت النِّسْوان. إمّ عُمر طلّعِت بِذِر مْخبّايْتُن مِن يوْم ما تركِت سورِيا: بندورة بلدية، خْيار، كوسا، وحبق. إمّ

حسن، يَلّي كانِت فِلّاحة بِحُمْص، شرحِت كيف لازِم يِزْرعوا حسب تِغْيير الطّقِس بِالبْقاع.

Once they had approval, the women gathered. Emm Omar brought out seeds she'd hidden since leaving Syria: local tomatoes, cucumbers, zucchini, and basil. Emm Hassan, who was a farmer in Homs, explained how they needed to plant according to the Bekaa's changing weather.

"هوْن غيْر عِنّا،" قالِت. "الصّيْف أقْسى والشِّتي أبْرد. لازِم نِخْتار الوَقِت المْناسِب لكِلّ نوْع."

"It's different here," she said. "The summer is harsher and the winter is colder. We must choose the right time for each type."

جابوا بْراميل قديمِة مِن مصْنع قريب، غسّلُوْن مْنيح، وعِمْلوا فِيُن فْخاويت للتِّصْريف. حطّوا بحْص تحِت، وجابوا تْراب مِن المزارِع القريبِة. كِلّ عيْلِة صار إلا برْميلين: واحد للْخُضْرا يَلّي بِتورِّق مِتِل الخسّ والِمْلوخية، وواحد للْخُضرا يَلّي بْتِطْول مِتِل البندورة والبامْيِة.

They got old barrels from a nearby factory, cleaned them thoroughly, and made drainage holes. They put gravel at the bottom and brought soil from nearby farms. Each family got two barrels: one for leafy vegetables like lettuce and molokhia, and one for tall vegetables like tomatoes and okra.

نورا نظّمِت جدْوَل لِلسّْقايِة. كِلّ عيْلِة مسْؤولة عن يوْم بِالْأُسْبوع، والِوْلاد بيساعْدوا بعِد ما يِرْجعوا مِن المدْرسِة. إمّ عُمر صارِت تْعلِّم البنات كيف يِخْتاروا البِذِر المْنيح ويْخزْنوا للمَوْسم الجايّ.

Noura organized a watering schedule. Each family is responsible for one day a week, and the children help after returning from school. Emm Omar started teaching the girls how to select good seeds and store them for next season.

"هَيْدا مِش بسّ مشْروع زِراعي،" قالِت نورا للشّاويش. "هَيْدا مشْروع أمل. عم نْعلِّم وْلادْنا إنّو في دايْماً فُرْصة نِخْلق شي حِلو، حتّى بِأصْعب الظّروف."

"This isn't just a gardening project," Noura told the Shawish. "This is a project of hope. We're teaching our children that there's always an opportunity to create something beautiful, even in the hardest circumstances."

بعِد شهِر، صار المشْروع حديث المُخيّم. النِّسْوان يَلّي ما شاركوا بِالْأوّل صاروا يِسْألوا إذا فِيْن يِنْضموا. حتّى بعْض العِيَل اللِّبْنانية مِن الضِّيَع القريبِة صاروا يوقفوا يِتْفرّجوا ويِسألوا عن الزِّراعة.

After a month, the project became the talk of the settlement. Women who hadn't participated at first started asking if they could join. Even some Lebanese families from the nearby village would stop to watch and ask about the gardening.

مرّة، إجِت مْوَظّفة مِن جمْعيةْ إغاثِة. شافِت المشْروع ونْبسطِت. قالِت: "فينا نْأمِنْلْكُن بْذور وأدَوات لِلْمَوْسم الجاي."

Once, an aid organization worker visited. She saw the project and was delighted. She said, "We can provide seeds and tools for next season."

بسّ التّحدِيات ما خِلْصِت. بِعزّ الصّيْف، صار في نقِص بِالْميّ. النِّسْوان جْتمعوا وقرّروا يِسْتعِمْلوا مَيّ الجلي والغسيل لسْقايِةْ النّباتات. وعِمْلوا شبكِةْ "تِنْقيط" بسيطة مِن قناني بْلاسْتيك قديمِة.

But the challenges weren't over. In mid-summer, there was a water shortage. The women gathered and decided to use grey water from washing dishes and clothes to water the plants. They created a simple drip irrigation system from old plastic bottles.

"شوفوا،" قالِت إمّ حسن لِلوْلاد وهِيِّ عم تِشْرحْلُن. "هيْك الميّ بْتِنْزل شْوَيّ شْوَيْ، وما بِتْضيع. هَيْدا مِن أسْرار الزِّراعة بِأرِض ناشْفِة."

"Look," Emm Hassan explained to the children. "This way the water drips slowly and doesn't go to waste. This is one of the secrets of farming in dry land."

مع الوَقِت، صار بيْن البْراميل مقاعِد مِن الخشب القديم. النِّسْوان بْيِجْتِمْعوا، بْيِشْربوا شاي، وبْيِحْكوا عن بلدُن وعن الزِّراعة. البنات الِصْغار صاروا يعِرْفوا أسامي كِلّ النّباتات، ويْميْزوا البِذِر.

Over time, benches made from old wood appeared between the barrels. Women would gather, drink tea, and talk about their homeland and farming. The young girls learned to identify all the plants and recognize the seeds.

وبِآخر المَوْسم، إمّ عُمر جمّعِت البنات وعلّمِتُن كيف يْخزْنوا البِذِر. "هَيْدي بْدور مِن بلدْنا،" قالِت. "لازِم نْحافِظ عْليا مِتِل ما حافظِت سِتّاتْنا عْلَيا مِن زمان."

At the end of the season, Emm Omar gathered the girls and taught them how to save seeds. "These are seeds from our homeland," she said. "We must preserve them just as our grandmothers preserved them long ago."

مشْروع الحديقة

ما حدا بْيِتْخيّل إنّو مشْروع زِراعي صْغير مُمْكِن يْغيِّر وِجّ مُخيّم كامِل، بسّ هَيْدا يَلّي صار بمُخيّم العَوْدِة بِسهْل البْقاع. المُخيّم، مِتِل غيْرو مِن المُخيّمات، كان مُجرّد تجمُّع خِيَم على أرْض مِسْتأجْرة، تحِت سما بْتعْرِف أقْسى درجات الحرارة صيْفاً وأبْرد العواصِف بِالشِّتي.

نورا الِحْسيْن، يَلّي حِمْلِت شْهادِةْ الهنْدسِة الزِّراعية مِن جامْعِةْ حلب، كانِت عم تْراقِب التِّغْيير الفصْلي للْأرِض الفاضْيَة بيْن الخِيَم. "كِلّ هالْأرِض، وعم نِشْتْري البندورة بِألْفيْن ليرة للْكيلو،" همسِت لحالا وهِيِّ واقْفِة قِدّام خيْمِتا، عْيونا على قُطْعِة الأرِض يَلّي ما فِيا شي غيْر شْوَيِّةْ حْجار وعِلب فاضْيِة.

بسّ المِشْكْلِة ما كانِت بِالْأرْض. أيّ مشْروع بِالْمُخيّم بْيِحْتاج مُوافقات مِن جِهّات كْتيرِة: الشّاويش عادِل، مسْؤول المُخيّم غيْر الرّسْمي؛ أبو غسّان، المُزارِع اللِّبْناني يَلّي مْأجّر الأرِض؛ البلدية يَلّي ما بِتْحِبّ تْشوف أيّ شي "دايِم" بِالْمُخيّمات؛ وكمان المُنظّمات الإنْسانية يَلّي بْتِشْرُف على المُخيّم.

"ليْش كِلّ هالتِّعْقيد؟" سألِت إمّ عُمر، يَلّي كانِت جارِةْ نورا وصديقِتا القريبِة. "يا ريْت المَوْضوع بسيط،" جاوبِتا نوْرا. "بسّ نِحْنا هوْن مِش على أرِضْنا. وكِلّ خُطْوِة لازِم تْكون مدْروسِة."

The Garden Project

No one imagines that a small agricultural project could change the face of an entire refugee settlement, but that's what happened at Al-Awda settlement in the Bekaa Valley. The settlement, like others, was merely a collection of tents on rented land, under skies that knew the harshest summer temperatures and the coldest winter storms.

Noura Al-Hussein, who held an agricultural engineering degree from Aleppo University, had been observing the seasonal changes of the empty land between the tents. "All this land, and we're buying tomatoes for 2,000 lira per kilo," she whispered to herself while standing in front of her tent, her eyes on the plot of land that held nothing but some stones and empty cans.

But the problem wasn't with the land. Any project in the settlement needed approvals from multiple parties: Shawish Adel, the informal settlement leader; Abu Ghassan, the Lebanese farmer who rented out the land; the municipality that didn't like seeing anything "permanent" in the settlements; and also the humanitarian organizations overseeing the settlement.

"Why all this complexity?" asked Emm Omar, who was Noura's neighbor and close friend. "If only it were simple," Noura replied. "But we're not on our own land here. Every step must be carefully considered."

بعِد شهِر مِن المُفاوضات، وإجْتِماعات مع كِلّ الجِهّات المعْنية، صار في إتِّفاق مكْتوب. المشْروع مسْموح بسّ بِشْروط: كِلّ شي لازِم يْكون قابِل للنّقِل، ممْنوع البِنا الثّابِت أَوْ حفْر الأرِض، الميّ بسّ مِن البير المْخصّص للمُخيّم، وأيّ محاصيل زْيادِة عن حاجِةْ العِيَل ممْنوع بيْعا بِالسّوق.

نورا ما زِعْلِت مِن الشّْروط. "القْيود بْتِخْلق الإبْداع،" قالِت بِإجْتِماع النِّسْوان الأوّل. عِشْرين مرا جْتمعوا بِخيْمِةْ إمّ عُمر، كِلّ وِحْدِة معا خِبْرِتا وقُصِّتا. إمّ حسن، يَلّي كانِت مُزارْعة بِحُمُص، جابِت معا دفْتر قديم مِلْيان مُلاحظات عن مَواسِم الزِّراعة. "هَيْدا دفْتر بيّي، الله يِرْحموا. كان يِكْتُب كِلّ شي عن الزِّراعة."

الفِكْرة الأساسية كانِت بسيطة: بْراميل بْلاسْتيك كْبيرِة للزِّراعة، بسّ التِّنْفيذ كان مِحْتاج تِخْطيط دقيق. كِلّ عيْلِة رح يْكون عِنْدا برْميلين، وكِلّ برْميل لازِم يْكون عِنْدو نِظام تِصْريف مْنيح ونِظام ريّ بسيط. الميّ، المَوْرد النّادِر بِالْمُخيّم، لازِم يُسْتعْمل بِحِكْمِة.

نادْيَه، بِنِت نورا الِصّْغيرِة، صارِت تْسجِّل كِلّ شي بِدفْترا المدْرسي. "ماما، ليْش عم تْحطوا بحِص بِكعْب البرْميل؟" سألِت وَقْتا كانوا عم يْجهْزوا أوّل دِفْعِةْ بْراميل. "كِرْمال الميّ تْصرِّف مْنيح،" شرحِتْلا إمّ حسن. "وكمان مِشان الجْذور ما تْعفِّن."

مع الوَقِت، المشْروع صار أكْبر مِن مُجرّد زِراعِةْ خُضْرا. صار مدْرسِة صْغيرِة مفْتوحة. النِّسْوان الِكْبار بيعلْموا البنات الِصْغار أسْرار الزِّراعة، والبنات عم يِتْعلّموا شي أكْبر مِن الزِّراعة: عم يِتْعلّموا إنّو المعْرِفة قُوِّة، وإنّو التّقاليد القديمِة فِيا حِكْمِة، وإنّو العمل الجّماعي بْيِخْلق المُعْجِزات.

After a month of negotiations and meetings with all concerned parties, a written agreement was reached. The project was permitted but with conditions: everything must be movable, no permanent construction or digging in the ground, water only from the settlement's designated well, and any surplus produce couldn't be sold in the market.

Noura wasn't upset by the conditions. "Constraints create creativity," she said at the first women's meeting. Twenty women gathered in Emm Omar's tent, each bringing her expertise and story. Emm Hassan, who had been a farmer in Homs, brought an old notebook full of notes about growing seasons. "This was my father's notebook, may God rest his soul. He wrote down everything about farming."

The basic idea was simple: large plastic barrels for planting, but the implementation needed precise planning. Each family would have two barrels, and each barrel needed to have a good drainage system and simple irrigation. Water, the scarce resource in the settlement, had to be used wisely.

Nadia, Noura's young daughter, started recording everything in her school notebook. "Mama, why are you putting gravel at the bottom of the barrel?" she asked the day they were preparing the first batch of barrels. "So the water drains well," Emm Hassan explained to her. "And also so the roots don't rot."

Over time, the project became more than just growing vegetables. It became a small open school. The older women taught the young girls the secrets of agriculture, and the girls were learning something bigger than farming: they were learning that knowledge is power, that old traditions hold wisdom, and that collective work creates miracles.

التّحدِّيات ما كانِت بسيطة. بِعِزّ الصّيْف، لمّا الشّمِس كانِت عم تِحْرُق الأرِض، واجهوا مِشْكْلِةْ نقص الميّ. بسّ الحلّ إجا مِن غيْر ما حدا يِتْوقّعو. أبو مالِك، جار لِبْناني مِن الضّيْعة القريبِة، شاف المشْروع ونْبسط مِن التّنْظيم والجِدّية. قال للشّاويش عادِل: "في عِنْدي بير قديم، ما عم نِسْتعمِلا. إذا بدّكُن تْمِدّو خط ميّ مِنّو، أنا ما عِنْدي مانِع."

هالْمُبادرة فتحِت باب جْديد. صار في تَواصُل بيْن نِسْوان المُخيّم والضّيْعة. إمّ مالِك، مرت أبو مالِك، صارِت تِحْضر إجْتماعات النِّسْوان وتِتْبادل الخُبُرات معُن. "زِراعِتْنا وِحْدِة،" قالِت. "وأرِضْنا وِحْدِة."

بِالْخريف، لمّا صارِت الغلِّة مْنيحة، نظّموا معْرض صْغير. حطّوا طاوْلات بيْن البِراميل، وعرضوا المونِة يَلّي عِمْلُوَا: مكْدوس باتِنْجان، كبيس خْيار، دِبس بندورة. كمان عِمْلوا رِكِن خاصّ للْبذور البلدية: بندورة حلبية، خْيار بلدي، مْلوخية حُمْصية. كِلّ نوْع بِقْزازة صْغيرِة، مع شرِح عن تاريخو وطريقِةْ زِراعْتو.

"شِفْتي شو عْمِلْتي؟" قال الشّاويش عادِل لنورا وهُوِّ عم يِتْفرّج على المعْرض. "خلقْتي جِسِر بيْن الماضي والحاضِر."

بسّ نورا كانِت عم تْفكِّر بِالْمُسْتقْبل. "المشْروع مِش بسّ للْأكِل،" قالِت. "عم نِزْرع أمل. كِلّ بِذْرة عم نْخبِّيا للْمَوْسم الجاي هِيِّ وعِد إنّو بُكْرا في فُرْصة نِرْجع نِزْرع مِن جْديد."

بْيوْم مِن أيّام الشِّتي، وبسّ كانِت نورا قاعْدِة مع نادْيَة بِنْتا عم تِفْرز بِذِر البندورة، سألِتا نادْيَة: "ماما، ليْش مِنْحُطّ كِلّ هالجِّهِد بِأرْض مِش إلْنا؟"

The challenges weren't simple. In mid-summer, when the sun was scorching the earth, they faced a water shortage. But the solution came unexpectedly. Abu Malek, a Lebanese neighbor from the nearby village, saw the project and was impressed by its organization and seriousness. He told Shawish Adel, "I have an old well we're not using. If you want to extend a water line from it, I have no objection."

This initiative opened a new door. Communication began between the women of the settlement and the village. Emm Malek, Abu Malek's wife, started attending the women's meetings and exchanging expertise with them. "Our agriculture is one," she said. "And our land is one."

In autumn, when the harvest was good, they organized a small exhibition. They set up tables between the barrels and displayed their preserved foods: makdous eggplant, pickled cucumbers, tomato molasses. They also created a special corner for local seeds: Aleppo tomatoes, baladi cucumbers, Homsi molokhia. Each variety in a small jar, with an explanation of its history and growing method.

"See what you've created?" Shawish Adel said to Noura as he looked at the exhibition. "You've built a bridge between past and present."

But Noura was thinking about the future. "The project isn't just for food," she said. "We're planting hope. Every seed we save for next season is a promise that tomorrow brings another chance to plant anew."

One winter day, while Noura was sitting with her daughter Nadia sorting tomato seeds, Nadia asked, "Mama, why do we put all this effort into land that isn't ours?"

نورا سكتِت شْوَيّ، وبعْديْن جاوَبِت: "بْتعِرْفي يا حبيبْتي، الفِلّاح الحقيقي بيحِبّ الأرِض حتّى لَوْ ما كانِت إلو. وكِلّ ما زْرِعْنا شي حِلو، مْنِتْرُك أثر مْنيح بِهالْعالم. يِمْكِن بُكْرا مِنْكون بِبلد تاني، بسّ الِمْهِمّ إنّو تعلّمْنا نِخْلق الحَياةْ ويْن ما كِنّا."

هلّأ، بعِد سِنِة مِن المشْروع، صار مُخيّم العَوْدِة معْروف بِحديقْتو. المنظّمات الإنْسانية بِتْجيب زُوّار يِتْفرّجوا على التّجْرِبِة، والجيران اللِّبْنانِيّين صاروا شُركا بِالْمعْرِفِة والخِبْرة. وأهمّ شي، صار في جيل جْديد مِن البنات والصّبايا بْيِعرْفوا قيمِةْ الأرِض والزِّراعة.

كِلّ ما حدا بْيِسْأل نورا: "وبعْديْن؟ شو المُسْتقْبل؟" بِتْجاوب: "المُسْتقْبل عم يِكْبر بِهالِبْراميل. عم نِزْرع خُضرا، بسّ عم نُحْصد أمل."

Noura was quiet for a moment, then answered, "You know, my darling, a true farmer loves the land even if it doesn't belong to them. And whenever we plant something beautiful, we leave a good mark on this world. Maybe tomorrow we'll be in another country, but what matters is that we learned to create life wherever we are."

Now, a year into the project, Al-Awda settlement has become known for its garden. Humanitarian organizations bring visitors to see the experience, and Lebanese neighbors have become partners in knowledge and expertise. Most importantly, there's a new generation of girls and young women who know the value of land and agriculture.

Whenever someone asks Noura, "What next? What's the future?" she answers, "The future is growing in these barrels. We're planting vegetables, but harvesting hope."

بِسِرّ السّاعاتي

The Watchmaker's Secret

Set in the final days of the French Mandate in Lebanon, this story weaves together the personal and political through the delicate work of a ساعاتي *sē3āti* (watchmaker). In 1943 Beirut's ancient souks, where gold merchants and craftsmen worked side by side, every shop held its secrets. But what happens when an elderly craftsman, bound by professional ethics to keep his customers' secrets, discovers that someone is using his respected profession for dangerous political purposes? Through the precision tools and quiet wisdom of a traditional watchmaker, we explore questions of loyalty, ضمير *ḍamīr* (conscience), and the subtle ways people resist occupation.

Key Vocabulary

- أفندي (*ʔafánadi*) – effendi (title of respect)
- أمانِة (*ʔamēni*) – trustworthiness
- إنْتِداب (*ʔintidēb*) – mandate
- تجسُّس (*tajássus*) – espionage
- تِلْميذ (*tilmīz*) – apprentice
- دُكّان/محلّ (*dukkēn/maɦáll*) – shop
- رِسالِة مْشفّرة (*risēli mšáffara*) – coded message
- زبون (*zabūn*) – customer
- سِرّ (*sirr*) – secret
- سوق الصّاغة (*sūʔ iṣṣāɣa*) – jewelers' souk/market
- شُرْطة (*šúrṭa*) – police
- ضابِط (*ḍābiṭ*) – officer
- مِحْتِرِف (*miɦtíraf*) – professional
- مُسْيو (*[monsieur]*)– mister
- مْعلِّم (*m3állim*) – master craftsman
- مُقاوَمة (*muʔēwami*) – resistance
- مِهْنِة (*míhni*) – profession, trade

The Watchmaker's Secret	***sirr issē3āti***	**سِرّ السّاعاتي**
Ibrahim is a watchmaker in old Beirut. He is seventy years old and knows how to fix all watches.	*brāhīm sē3āti bi-bayrūt ilʔadīmi. 3úmru sab3īn síni u byá3rif yṣálliħ kill issē3āt.*	إبْراهيم ساعاتي بِبَيْروت القديمِة. عُمْرو سبْعين سِنِة وبْيَعْرِف يْصلِّح كِلّ السّاعات.
On Thursday, a strange man brought a watch to the shop. He said, "I want it tomorrow."	*yōm ilxamīs, zálami ɣarīb jēb sē3a 3a -lmaħáll. ʔāl: "báddi yēha búkra."*	يوْم الخميس، زلمي غريب جاب ساعة عَ المحلّ. قال: "بدّي ياها بُكْرا."
Ibrahim opened the watch. He found a small paper inside. The paper had secret numbers and words.	*brāhīm fátaħ issē3a. lēʔa wárʔa ṣɣīri júwwa. -lwárʔa fíya ʔarʔām u kilmēt sirríyyi.*	إبْراهيم فتح السّاعة. لاقى وَرْقة صْغيرِة جُوّا. الوَرْقة فِيا أرْقام وكِلْمات سِرّية.
He went to his friend Omar. Omar said, "This is an important and dangerous message!"	*rāħ 3ind rfīʔu 3úmar. 3úmar ʔāl: "hēy risēli mhímmi u xaṭíra!"*	راح عِنْد رْفيقو عُمر. عُمر قال: "هاي رِسالِة مْهِمِّة وخطيرة!"

Then, a French officer came to the shop. He asked about the watch and the strange man.	*ba3dēn, ʔija ḍābiṭ frinsēwi 3a -lmaɧáll. sáʔal 3an issē3a u 3an izzálami -lɣarīb.*	بعْديْن، إجا ضابِط فْرِنْساوي عَ المحلّ. سأل عن السّاعة وعن الزّلمي الغريب.
Ibrahim fixed the watch and left the paper in its place. He didn't tell anyone about the secret.	*brāhīm ṣállaɧ issē3a u xálla -lwárʔa maɧálla. ma xábbar ɧáda 3an issirr.*	إبْراهيم صلّح السّاعة وخلّى الوَرْقة محلّا. ما خبّر حدا عن السِّرّ.

A2

The Watchmaker's Secret

سِرّ السّاعاتي

Beirut, 1943. Ibrahim's watch shop in the Jewelers' Souk hasn't changed in forty years. The shop is small but full of old watches and precise tools.

بَيْروت، ١٩٤٣. محلّ إبْراهيم السّاعاتي بِسوق الصّاغة ما تْغيّر مِن أرْبْعين سِنِة. المحلّ صْغير، بسّ مِلْيان ساعات قديمِة وأدَوات دقيقة.

Ibrahim, who is seventy years old, is known for his precise work. Every day he opens his shop at seven and sits behind his ancient wooden table.

إبْراهيم، يَلّي عُمْرو سبْعين سِنِة، معْروف بِشِغْلو الدّقيق. كِلّ يوْم بْيِفْتح محلّو السّاعة سبْعة، وبْيِقْعُد وَرا طاوِلْتو الخشب العتيقة.

On Thursday, a strange man came to the shop. He wore an elegant suit and spoke French. He said, "I need to fix this watch. I want it tomorrow."

يوْم الخميس، إجا زلمي غريب عَ المحلّ. لابِس بدْلِة مْرتّبِة وبْيِحْكي فْرِنْساوي. قال: "بدّي صلِّح هالسّاعة. بُكْرا بدّي ياها."

Ibrahim opened the watch and found a small paper hidden inside. It had numbers and letters he didn't understand. "Strange," Ibrahim thought. "This is the third watch this month with a paper."

إبْراهيم فتح السّاعة وشاف وَرْقة صْغيرِة مْخِبّايِة جُوّا. عْلَيا أرْقام وحْروف ما فِهِما. "غريب،" فكّر إبْراهيم. "هاي تالِت ساعة هالشِّهِر فِيا وَرْقة."

The next day, a French officer came to the shop. He asked about the man and the watch. Ibrahim became scared. What was in these papers?	تاني يوْم، إجا ضابِط فْرِنْساوي عَ المحلّ. سأل عن الزّلمي وعن السّاعة. إبْراهيم خاف. شو في بِهالِوْراق؟
He decided to go to his old friend, Omar Effendi, who worked at the post office. Omar read the paper and his face turned white. “Ibrahim! This is a coded message. They’re reporting information about army movements!”	قرّر يْروح عِنْد رْفيقو القديم، عُمر أفنْدي، يَلّي كان يِشْتِغِل بِالْبريد. عُمر قُري الوَرْقة وصار وِجّو أبْيَض: ”إبْراهيم! هَيْدي رِسالِة مْشفّرة. عم يْخبْروا مْعْلومات عن تحرُّكات الجيْش!”
Ibrahim returned to his shop with his heart pounding. What should he do? Report to the authorities or protect his customers?	إبْراهيم رِجِع عَ محلّو وقلْبو بيدِقّ. شو لازِم يَعْمُل؟ يْخبِّر السُّلْطات وَلّا يِحْمي زبايْنو؟

سِرّ السّاعاتي

The Watchmaker's Secret

بَيْروت، خريف ١٩٤٣. الشّمِس عم تْغيب على سوق الصّاغة، وإبْراهيم السّاعاتي عم يِتْأمّل بِالسّاعة يَلّي قِدّامو. أرْبْعين سِنِة وهُوِّ بيصلِّح السّاعات بِهالْمحلّ الِصّْغير، وما مرِّت عْليْه ساعة غريبِة مِتِل هاي.

Beirut, autumn 1943. The sun is setting over the Jewelers' Souk, and Ibrahim the watchmaker is examining the watch in front of him. For forty years, he has been repairing watches in this small shop, and he's never seen a strange watch like this one.

"إذا بْتِخْلص بُكْرا، بِدْفعْلك ضُعْفيْن،" هيْك قال الزُّبون الِمْرتّب يَلّي جاب السّاعة. كان لابِس بدْلِة إنْكْليزية غالْيِة، وساعِةْ روْليْكْس بِإيدو الِشّْمال، بسّ لهِجْتو الفْرِنْساوية ما كانِت طبيعية.

"If you finish it tomorrow, I'll pay you double," said the elegant customer who brought the watch. He wore an expensive English suit and a Rolex watch on his left wrist, but his French accent wasn't natural.

إبْراهيم، يَلّي تْعلّم المِهْنِة على إيد مْعلّْمو بِإسْطنْبول، بْيَعْرِف إنّو السّاعة مِش بسّ آلِة لقْياس الوَقِت. "السّاعة بْتِحْكي قِصِّةْ صاحِبا،" هيْك كان يْقول. وهالسّاعة عم تِحْكي قِصّة غريبِة.

Ibrahim, who learned his craft from his master in Istanbul, knows that a watch isn't just a device for measuring time. "A watch tells its owner's story," he would say. And this watch was telling a suspicious story.

تحْت قْزاز السّاعة، لاقى وَرْقة مُطْوية بِعِنايِة. أرْقام وحْروف مكْتوبِة بِخطّ دقيق: B-4-17، غداً، ميناء ٣. هاي تالِت ساعة هالشّهِر فِيا رسايِل مْشفّرة.

Under the watch glass, he found a carefully folded paper. Numbers and letters written in precise handwriting: "B-4-17, tomorrow, Port 3." This was the third watch this month containing coded messages.

"يا ترى شو عم يْصير بِهالْبلد؟" سأل حالو هُوِّ وعم يِتْذكّر الأحْداث الأخيرة. الِفْرِنْساوِيّين مِتْوَتّْرين، والوَطنِيّين اللّبْنانِيّين عم يْطالْبوا بِالْإسْتِقلال. كِلّ شي عم يِغْلي تحِت السّطح.

"I wonder what's happening in this country?" he asked himself, remembering recent events. The French are tense, and Lebanese nationalists are demanding independence. Everything is boiling under the surface.

قرّر يْزور رْفيقو القديم، عُمر أفنْدي، يَلّي كان يِشْتِغِل بِالْبريد المرْكزي. عُمر كان معْروف بِمعْرِفْتو بِالسِّياسِة وأخْبار البلد. بعِد ما قرا الوَرْقة، صار وِجّ عُمر أبْيَض مِتِل الِطّحين.

He decided to visit his old friend, Omar Effendi, who worked at the central post office. Omar was known for his knowledge of politics and country news. After reading the paper, Omar's face turned white as flour.

"إبْراهيم، هَيْدي مِش شغْلِة بسيطة. هَيْدوْل معْلومات عن تحرُّكات عسْكرية. في ناس عم تْراقِب تحرُّكات الجيْش الفرنْسي."

"Ibrahim, this isn't a simple matter. This is information about military movements. People are monitoring French army movements."

"شو المطْلوب مِنّي؟" سأل إبْراهيم.

"What am I supposed to do?" asked Ibrahim.

"نْتِبِهْ! الفْرِنْساوِيّين ما بْيِرْحموا حدا بيساعِد المُقاومِة. وإذا خبّرْتُن، رح تِخْسر ثِقِةْ النّاس فيك."

"Be careful! The French don't show mercy to anyone who helps the resistance. And if you tell them, you'll lose people's trust in you."

رِجِع إبْراهيم عَ المحلّ وراسو مِلْيان أفْكار. تْذكّر كيف بَيّو كان يْقول: "السّاعاتي مُؤْتمن على أسْرار زبايْنو مِتِل الحكيم."

Ibrahim returned to the shop with his head full of thoughts. He remembered how his father used to say, "A watchmaker is entrusted with his customers' secrets like a doctor."

بسّ هالْمرّة السِّرّ أكْبر مِن سِرّ شخْصي. بُكْرا رح يِرْجع الزّْبون ياخُد السّاعة، والضّابِط الفْرِنْساوي يَلّي مرق الصُّبُح أكيد رح يِرْجع كمان.

But this time the secret was bigger than a personal one. Tomorrow the customer would return for the watch, and the French officer who passed by in the morning would surely return too.

فجْأة، سِمِع دقّ على باب المحلّ. كان المُسْيو جان، صاحِب القهْوِة القريبِة. "مُسْيو إبْراهيم، في ضُبّاط فْرِنْساوِيّين عم يِسْألوا عنّك وعن محلّك."

Suddenly, he heard a knock on the shop door. It was Monsieur Jean, the owner of the nearby café. "Monsieur Ibrahim, there are French officers asking about you and your shop."

إبْراهيم سكّر محلّو بْسِرْعة وراح على بَيْتو بِطريقة خلْفية. طول اللّيْل ما نام، عم يْفكِّر شو لازِم يَعْمُل. السّاعة كانِت معو بِالْبيْت.

Ibrahim quickly closed his shop and went home through a back road. All night he couldn't sleep, thinking about what he should do. The watch was with him at home.

الصُّبْح، قبِل ما يِطْلع الضّوْ، راح عِنْد خيُّو الِكْبير، يوسِف، تاجِر القْماش المعْروف. يوسِف سِمْعو بِهْدوء وبعْديْن قال: "في شي أهمّ مِن السِّياسِة: الضّمير. شو بيقِلّك ضميرك يا إبْراهيم؟"

Before sunrise, he went to his older brother Youssef, a well-known fabric merchant. Youssef listened quietly and then said, "There's something more important than politics: conscience. What does your conscience tell you, Ibrahim?"

إبْراهيم فكّر شْوَيّ. تْذكّر كيف الفْرِنْساوِيّين حبسوا إبِن جارو لِأنّو كتب مقال بيطالِب بِالْلإسْتِقْلال. وتْذكّر كمان كيف عيْلْتو عاشِت وَقِت العِثْمانِيّين والفْرِنْساوِيّين، وكيف النّاس دايْماً كانِت توثق في وبِمحلّو.

Ibrahim thought for a moment. He remembered how the French imprisoned his neighbor's son for writing an article demanding independence. He also remembered how his family had lived through Ottoman and French rule, and how people had always trusted him and his shop.

رِجِع عَ المحلّ. فتح السّاعة، صلّحا مْنيح، وحطّ الوَرْقة محلّا. ما حدا بْيِقْدر يْقول إنّو ما عِمِل شِغْلو بِأمانِة.

He returned to the shop. He opened the watch, fixed it well, and left the paper where it was. No one could say he hadn't done his job faithfully.

بعِد الضُّهُر، رِجِع الزُّبون. عطا السّاعة وقال: "تْفضّل. مِتِل ما طلبِت، جاهْزة بِالْيوْم التّاني."

In the afternoon, the customer returned. He gave him the watch and said, "Here you are. As requested, ready the next day."

شْوَيّ بعْدا، إجا الضّابِط الفْرِنْساوي. سألو عن الزِّبون وعن السّاعة. إبْراهيم جاوَب بِبساطة: "كْتير ناس بْتِجي عِنْدي. ما بِتْذكّرْن كِلُّن."

Shortly after, the French officer came. He asked him about the customer and the watch. Ibrahim answered simply, "Many people come to me. I don't remember them all."

سِرّ السّاعاتي

خريف ١٩٤٣، بَيْروت القديمِة. شَوارِع سوق الصّاغة الضّيْقة ما بِتْخبّي بسّ محلّات الدّهب والفِضّة، بسّ كمان أسْرار المدينِة وحْكاياتا. بيْن هالدْكاكين العتيقة، في محلّ صْغير معْروف عِنْد الكِلّ: محلّ إبْراهيم السّاعاتي.

إبْراهيم، يَلّي تْخطّى السّبْعين، شاف بَيْروت عم تِتْغيّر قِدّام عَيْنو. مِن أيّام العِثْمانيين، للْحرْب العالمية، للْإنْتِداب الفرَنْساوي. شاف النّاس عم تِتْغيّر، والأزْياء عم تِتْبدّل، والسِّلْطات بِتْروح وبْتِجي، بسّ مِهْنتو ضلِّت مِتِل ما هِيِّ: دقيقة، وبْتِطلُب صبِر، ومِلْيانِة أسْرار.

"السّاعة بْتِحْكي قِصِّةْ صاحِبا،" هيْك كان يْقول لتِلْميذو فريد، إبِن خيّو يَلّي بلّش يِتْعلّم المِهْنة عِنْدو. "بْتِعْرِف مِن حركِةْ البنْدول إذا صاحِبا سريع وَلّا بطيء، ومِن الخدِش على العِلْبِة بْتِعْرِف إذا حريص وَلّا مُهْمِل."

هالصُّبُح، إجِت ساعة غريبِة. زلمي مْرتّب كْتير، بِلهْجِة فْرنْساوية مُصْطنْعة، طلب يْصلِّحا بِسِرْعة. "بُكْرا بِمْرُق ، وبِدْفعْلك ضُعفيْن."

بسّ فلّ الزّبون، فتح إبْراهيم السّاعة بِدِقّة. عْيونو المْدرّبِة مِن عشْرات السِّنين لمحِت مُباشرةً الوَرْقة المْخبّايِة تحت القِرِص. حْروف وأرْقام مكْتوبِة بِخطّ دقيق: B-4-17، بُكْرا، مينا ٣، شِحْنِة خاصّة.

تْنهّد إبْراهيم. هاي تالت مرّة هالشّهِر بْلاقي رسايِل مْشفّرة بِساعات زبايْنو. المرّة الأولى فكّر إنّا صُدْفِة. المرّة التّانْيِة صار عِنْدو شكّ. أمّا هلّأ، ما عاد في مجال للشكّ: محلّو صار مْحطة لتبادُل المعْلومات السِّرية.

The Watchmaker's Secret

Autumn 1943, Old Beirut. The narrow streets of the Jewelers' Souk hide not only shops of gold and silver but also the city's secrets and tales. Among these ancient shops stands a small store known to everyone: Ibrahim the watchmaker's shop.

Ibrahim, who had passed seventy, had watched Beirut change before his eyes. From Ottoman times, through the World War, to the French Mandate. He saw people change, fashions shift, and authorities come and go, but his profession remained the same: precise, requiring patience, and full of secrets.

"A watch tells its owner's story," he would say to his apprentice Farid, his nephew who had started learning the trade from him. "You can tell from the pendulum's movement if its owner is quick or slow, and from the scratches on the case if they're careful or careless."

This morning, a strange watch arrived. An elegant man, with an artificial French accent, asked to have it fixed quickly. "I'll pick it up tomorrow and pay you double."

After the customer left, Ibrahim carefully opened the watch. His eyes, trained by decades of experience, immediately spotted the paper hidden under the dial. Letters and numbers written in precise handwriting: "B-4-17, tomorrow, Port 3, special shipment."

Ibrahim sighed. This was the third time this month he had found coded messages in customers' watches. The first time, he thought it was a coincidence. The second time, he became suspicious. But now, there was no room for doubt: his shop had become a station for exchanging secret information.

عْيونو راحِت على صورِةْ بيّو الِمْعلّقة على الحيْط. حْسيْن السّاعاتي، يَلّي تْعلّم المِهْنِة بِإسْطنْبول وعلّما لإبْنو بِكِلّ أمانِة. "السّاعاتي مُؤْتمن على أسْرار زبايْنو مِتْل الحكيم،" كان يْقول. بسّ شو بيصير لمّا السِّرّ بْيِتْعلّق بِأمْن البلد كِلّو؟

قطع تِفْكيرو صوْت دقّ على الباب. كان المُسْيو جان، صاحِب القهْوِة الفِرِنْساوي يَلّي فتح قبِل سِنْتيْن على راس الزّْقاق. "مُسْيو إبْراهيم، في شي مْهِمّ لازِم تعِرْفو. في ضُبّاط فْرِنْساوِيّين عم يِسْألوا عنّك وعن محلّك."

"شو عم يْقولوا؟"

"ما بعْرف عَ المزْبوط، بسّ سْمِعْتُن عم يِحْكوا عن تجسُّس ومُقاوَمِة. نصيحة مِنّي: سكِّر محلّك اليوْم وروح عَ البيْت."

إبْراهيم سكّر المحلّ، بسّ ما راح عَ البيْت. مِشي بْشوارِع بَيْروت القديمِة يَلّي بْيِعْرِفا مِتِل كفّ إيدو، لحدّ ما وُصِل لمحلّ خيّو الِكْبير يوسِف.

يوسِف، تاجِر القْماش المعْروف، كان عِنْدو تجْرُبِة مع السِّياسِة. بِزمن العِثْمانِيّين، دفع تمن غالي لمّا رفض يْخبِّر السُّلْطات عن تُجّار كانوا بيهرْبوا السْلاح للثُّوّار العرب. تْعذّب بِالسِّجن شهْريْن، بسّ ما حِكي كِلْمِة.

"المَوْضوع خطير يا إبْراهيم،" قال يوسِف بعِد ما سِمِع القُصّة. "المُقاوَمِة عم تِسْتعْمِل شبكِة مْعقّدِة لنقِل المعْلومات. السّاعات فِكْرة ذكية... ما حدا بيشِك فِيا."

His eyes went to his father's picture hanging on the wall. Hussein the watchmaker, who learned the trade in Istanbul and taught it to his son with complete honesty. "A watchmaker is entrusted with his customers' secrets like a doctor," he used to say. But what happens when the secret concerns the security of the entire country?

His thoughts were interrupted by a knock on the door. It was Monsieur Jean, owner of the French café that opened two years ago at the top of the alley. "Monsieur Ibrahim, there's something important you should know. French officers are asking about you and your shop."

"What are they saying?"

"I'm not sure exactly, but I heard them talking about espionage and resistance. My advice: close your shop today and go home."

Ibrahim closed the shop, but didn't go home. He walked through the old Beirut streets he knew like the lines on his palm, until he reached his older brother Youssef's store.

Youssef, the well-known fabric merchant, had experience with politics. During Ottoman times, he paid a heavy price when he refused to inform authorities about merchants who were smuggling weapons to Arab rebels. He was tortured in prison for two months but never said a word.

"This is dangerous, Ibrahim," said Youssef after hearing the story. "The resistance is using a complex network to transfer information. Watches are a clever idea... no one suspects them."

"شو بْتعْمُل محلّي؟"

"مِش مْهِمّ شو كِنِت بعْمُل محلّك. المْهِمّ إنْتَ شو بدّك تعْمِل. بْتعْرِف؟ في شي أهمّ مِن السِّياسِة: الضّمير. شو بيقِلّك ضميرك؟"

إبْراهيم فكّر بِعُمُق. تْذكّر حكي مْعلّمو بِإسْطنْبول: "مِهْنِتْنا بِتْعلِّمْنا إنّو كِلّ قِطعْة صْغيرِة بِالسّاعة مْهِمّة. إذا خِرْبِت وِحْدِة، بْتوقف السّاعة كِلّا." وهيْك كمان البلد، كِلّ واحد عِنْدو دَوْرو.

قرّر يِرْجع عَ المحلّ. فتح السّاعة، صلّحا بِعِنايِة، وحطّ الوَرْقة محلّا. بسّ قبِل ما يْسكّرا، كتب بِقلم رْصاص رفيع على طرف الوَرْقة: "العيْن عْلَيْكُن."

بعِد الضُّهُر، رِجِع الزّبون. بسّ هالْمرّة، ما كان لَوَحْدو. في تْنيْن كانوا واقْفين بِالزّاوْيِة، عم يْراقبوا المحلّ.

"السّاعة جاهْزِة؟" سأل الزّبون.

"طبْعاً. بسّ قبِل ما أعْطيك ياها، عِنْدي سُؤال: مين علّمك تْحطّ الرّسايِل بِالسّاعات؟"

وِجّ الزّبون صار أبْيَض. "ما بعْرِف عن شو عم تِحْكي..."

"أنا ساعاتي مِن خمْسين سِنِة. السّاعة بْتِحْكي قِصّةْ صاحِبا، وساعْتك عم تِحْكي قِصّةْ مِش بسّ قِصْتك."

فجْأة، دخل الضّابِط الفرِنْساوي للْمحلّ. "مْسيو إبْراهيم، نِحْنا عم نْراقِب محلّك مِن فتْرة..."

"وأنا عم راقِب السّاعات يَلّي عم تِجيني،" قاطعو إبْراهيم. "وعِنْدي لايْحة بِكِلّ السّاعات يَلّي شِفْتا مِن شهِر، وكِلّ يَلّي جابُوا. بِتْحبّوا تْشوفوه؟"

"What would you do in my place?"

"It's not important what I would do in your place. What's important is what you want to do. You know? There's something more important than politics: conscience. What does your conscience tell you?"

Ibrahim thought deeply. He remembered what his master in Istanbul used to say, "Our profession teaches us that every small piece in the watch is important. If one breaks, the whole watch stops." And so it is with the country, everyone has their role.

He decided to return to the shop. He opened the watch, fixed it carefully, and put the paper back in its place. But before closing it, he wrote in thin pencil on the edge of the paper "Eyes are on you."

In the afternoon, the customer returned. But this time, he wasn't alone. Two men were standing in the corner, watching the shop.

"Is the watch ready?" asked the customer.

"Of course. But before I give it to you, I have a question: who taught you to put messages in watches?"

The customer's face turned white. "I don't know what you're talking about..."

"I've been a watchmaker for fifty years. A watch tells its owner's story, and your watch is telling a story that isn't yours."

Suddenly, the French officer entered the shop. "Monsieur Ibrahim, we've been monitoring your shop for a while..."

"And I've been monitoring the watches that come to me," Ibrahim interrupted. "And I have a list of every watch I've seen this month, and everyone who brought them. Would you like to see it?"

الضّابِط والِزّْبون تْبادلوا نظرات قلق.

"خود السّاعة،" قال إبْراهيم. "بسّ تْذكّر: مِتِل ما السّاعة ما بْتِمْشي إلّا بْتعاوُن كِلّ قُطعا، البلد ما بْيِمْشي إلّا لمّا نِتْعاون كِلّْنا. وأنا، مِتِل هالسّاعة، بْضلّ أمين على الوَقِت... ووَقْت الحُرّية إجا."

مِن هَيْداك اليوْم، ما حدا جاب ساعة فِيا رسايِل لإبْراهيم. بسّ النّاس ضلِّت تِحْكي عن السّاعاتي يَلّي حافظ على سِرّ المُقاوَمة وسِرّ المِهْنِة بِنفْس الوَقِت.

The officer and the customer exchanged worried looks.

“Take the watch,” said Ibrahim. “But remember: just as a watch doesn’t work without the cooperation of all its parts, a country doesn’t work until we all cooperate. And I, like this watch, remain faithful to time... and the time for freedom has come.”

From that day on, no one brought watches with messages to Ibrahim. But people continued to talk about the watchmaker who preserved both the resistance’s secret and the honor of his profession at the same time.

صوْت وصورة

Sound and Image

In the vibrant world of Lebanese weddings, where tradition meets modernity, two artists find themselves repeatedly crossing paths: a مْصوِّرة *mṣáwwira* (photographer) with an eye for candid moments and a مُغنّي *muɣánni* (singer) devoted to classical أغاني *ʔaɣāni* (songs). While he fills wedding halls with the warmth of traditional لحْن *laħn* (melodies), she captures the fleeting لحْظات *laħẓēt* (moments) that tell each عِرس *3íris* (wedding)'s unique story. Their initial quarrels – him annoyed by her camera's intrusion, her frustrated by his rigid adherence to tradition – gradually transform into something unexpected as they learn to see the beauty of حفْلات *ħaflēt* (celebrations) through each other's eyes. But in a culture where both الصُّوَر *iṣṣúwar* (photographs) and الموسيقى *ilmūsīʔa* (music) are considered essential to preserving memories, can these two artists find harmony in their different approaches to capturing love?

Key Vocabulary

- أُغْنية (*ʔuɣníyyi*) – song
- حُبّ (*ɦubb*) – love
- رقص (*ráʔiṣ*) – dance
- زَواج (*zawēj*) – marriage
- عازِف (*3āzif*)– musician
- عروس (*3arūs*) – bride
- عريس (*3arīs*) – groom
- قِصّة (*ʔíṣṣa*) – story
- كاميرا (*kēmira*) – camera
- كوْرْنيش (*kōrnīš*) – seaside promenade
- لحْن (*laɦn*) – melody
- مسْرح (*másraɦ*) – stage
- معْرض (*má3raḍ*) – exhibition

Sound and Image	*ṣōt u ṣūra*	صوْت وصورة
Hana is a wedding photographer. She loves photographing people when they are happy.	*hána mṣáwwrit ʔa3rās. híyyi bitɦíbb tṣáwwir innēs hínni u mabsūṭīn.*	هنا مْصَوِّرِةْ أعْراس. هِيِّ بِتْحِبّ تْصوِّر النّاس هِنّي ومبْسوطين.
Ghassan is a wedding singer. His voice is very beautiful and everyone loves to hear him.	*ɣassān biɣánni bi-lʔa3rās. ṣáwtu ɦílu ktīr u kill innēs biɦíbbu yisma3ū.*	غسّان بيغنّي بِالْأعْراس. صَوْتو حِلو كْتير وكِلّ النّاس بيحِبّوا يِسْمعوه.
When they first met, they didn't like each other. She stood in front of him while he was singing, and he got angry with her.	*ʔáwwal ma tlēʔu, ma ɦábbu ba3ḍ. híyyi wíʔfit ʔiddēmu húwwi u 3am yɣánni, u húwwi zí3il mínna.*	أوّل ما تْلاقوا، ما حبّوا بعْض. هِيِّ وِقْفِت قِدّامو هُوِّ وعم يْغنّي، وهُوِّ زِعِل مِنّا.
But at every wedding, they started seeing each other. He heard how she talks about photos, and she heard how he sings.	*bass kill 3íris, ṣāru yšūfu ba3ḍ. húwwi sími3 kīf híyyi btíɦki 3an iṣṣúwar, u híyyi sím3it kīf húwwi biɣánni.*	بسّ كِلّ عِرس، صاروا يْشوفوا بعْض. هُوِّ سِمِع كيف هِيِّ بْتِحْكي عن الصُّوَر، وهِيِّ سِمْعِت كيف هُوِّ بيغنّي.

On Friday, Ghassan has a concert. He asked Hana, “Would you like to come listen?”	*yōm iljúm3a, ɣassān 3índu ɦáfli. sáʔal hána: “bitɦíbbi tiji tisma3īni?”*	يوْم الجُمْعة، غسّان عِنْدو حفْلِة. سأل هنا: "بِتْحِبّي تِجي تِسْمعيني؟"
Hana went to the concert. Ghassan sang the most beautiful songs. Then they walked together and talked a lot.	*rāɦit hána 3a -lɦáfli. ɣassān ɣánna ʔáɦla ʔaɣāni. ba3dēn míšyu sáwa u ɦíkyu ktīr.*	راحِت هنا عَ الحفْلِة. غسّان غنّى أحْلى أغاني. بعْديْن مِشْيوا سَوا وحِكْيوا كْتير.
Today, they are bride and groom. She didn’t carry her camera, and he sang only for her.	*-lyōm, hínni 3irsēn. híyyi ma ɦímlit ilkēmira, u húwwi ɣánna bass ʔíla.*	اليوْم، هِنّي عِرْسان. هِيِّ ما حِمْلِت الكاميرا، وهُوِّ غنّى بسّ إلا.

Sound and Image	صوْت وصورة
Hana is leaving a wedding party carrying her large camera. She was tired but happy. Her photos today were very beautiful.	هنا طالْعة مِن حفْلِةْ العِرِس هِيِّ وعم بِتْشيل كاميرْتا الكْبيرِة. كانِت تِعْبانة بسّ مبْسوطة. صُوَرا كْتير حِلْوِة اليوْم.
"I wish you'd pay attention to others!" an angry male voice came from behind her. It was Ghassan, the famous wedding singer in Beirut. "You stood in front of me three times today while I was singing!"	"يا ريْت تِنْتِبْهي شْوَيّ لغيْرِك!" صوْت رِجّالي عصبي مِن وَراها. كان غسّان، المُغنّي المشْهور بأعْراس بَيْروت. "وْقِّفْتي قِدّامي تْلات مرّات اليوْم أنا وعم غنّي!"
"What do you want? My job is to take pictures! And you blocked the path with your musicians!"	"شو بدّك؟ شِغْلي إنّي صوِّر! وإنْتَ سكّرْت الطّريق بِالْعازْفين تبعك!"
But Ghassan didn't hear her response. He was busy cleaning the coffee that spilled on his white shirt when he bumped into her.	بسّ غسّان ما سِمِع جَوابا. كان مشْغول بِتِمْسيح القهْوِة يَلّي نْكبِّت على قميصو الأبْيَض لمّا خبط فِيا.
The following week, Hana was surprised when she saw Ghassan at another wedding. This time, she heard him singing an old song with a very beautiful voice.	الأُسْبوع يَلّي بعْدو، تْفاجأِت هنا لمّا شافِت غسّان بْعِرِس تاني. هالْمرّة، سِمْعِتو عم يْغنّي غِنّية قديمِة بِصوْت حِلو كْتير.

“You sing well,” she told him while photographing the bride.	“بْتعْرِف تْغنّي مْنيح،” قالِتْلو هِيِّ وعم بِتْصوِّر العروس.
“And you take good photos,” he answered. “But you stand in wrong places!”	“وإنْتي بْتعِرْفي تْصوْري مْنيح،” جاوَبا. “بسّ بْتوقفي بِمحلّات غلط!”
They both laughed.	ضِحْكوا التّنيْن.
They started meeting every week at different weddings. Over time, they began talking more. She loved his way of singing old songs, and he enjoyed her artistic photos.	صاروا يِتْلاقوا كِلّ أُسْبوع بِأعْراس مِخْتِلْفِة. مع الوَقِت، بلّشوا يِحْكوا أكْتر. هِيِّ حبِّت كيف بيغنّي الأغاني القديمِة، وهُوِّ نْبسط مِن صُوَرا الفنّية.
On Friday, at the last wedding, Ghassan asked Hana to photograph him while singing. After the wedding, they sat and had coffee together.	يوْم الجُمْعة، بآخِر عِرِس، طلب غسّان مِن هنا تْصوْرو هُوِّ وعم يْغنّي. بعِد العِرِس، قعدوا يِشْربوا قهْوِة سَوا.
“You know?” said Ghassan. “When I first saw you, I thought you were annoying. But now I see weddings more beautifully through your camera lens.”	“بْتعِرْفي؟” قال غسّان. “أوّل ما شِفْتِك فكّرْتِك مِزْعِجِة. بسّ هلّأ بْشوف الأعْراس أحْلى مِن وَرا كاميرْتِك.”
“And I thought you were arrogant,” Hana laughed. “But now I love hearing you sing.”	“وأنا كِنِت مْفكّْرتِك مغْرور،” ضِحْكِت هنا. “بسّ هلّأ بْحِبّ إسْمعك عم تْغنّي.”

صوْت وصورة

Sound and Image

"بِدّي الصّورة تْكون مِخْتِلْفِة!" العروس عم تْصرِّخ وعْيونا مِلْيانِة دْموع. "كِلّ الصُوَر الأعْراس صارِت نفْس الشّي!"

"I want the photo to be different!" The bride is shouting with tears in her eyes. "All wedding photos have become the same!"

هنا حطِّت الكاميرا على جنب وغمرِت العروس. خمْس سْنين خِبْرة بِتِصْوير الأعْراس علّمِتا إنّو العروس بِهالْيوْم بِتْكون عم تِمْرُق بِألْف حالِة.

Hana put down her camera and hugged the bride. Five years of experience in wedding photography taught her that brides go through a thousand emotions on their wedding day.

"عِنْدي فِكْرة،" قالِت هنا. "بسّ بدُّنا مُساعدِةْ المُغنّي."

"I have an idea," said Hana. "But we need the singer's help."

"قصْدِك غسّان؟ هُوِّ مُسْتحيل يْغيِّر شي بِبِرْنامْجو!"

"You mean Ghassan? He never changes anything in his program!"

"خلِّيا عليّي."

"Leave it to me."

مِشْيِت هنا لعِنْد غسّان يَلّي كان عم يْجهِّز العازْفين تبعو. مِن شهْريْن وهِنّي عم يِتْلاقوا بِكِلّ عِرِس، وكِلّ مرّة بْيِتْخانقوا على شي: هُوِّ بدّو يْغنّي بِطريقْتو التّقْليدية، وهِيِّ بدّا تْصوِّر بِأفْكار جْديدِة.

Hana walked over to Ghassan, who was preparing his musicians. For two months, they had been meeting at every wedding, and each time they argued about something: he wanted to sing in his traditional way, and she wanted to photograph with new ideas.

"غسّان، بدّي مُساعدْتك."

"Ghassan, I need your help."

"شو؟ بدِّك تْصوّري قِدّامي بعِد مرّة؟" بسّ هالْمرّة، إبْتِسامِة صْغيرِة بيّنِت على وِجّو.

"What? Want to photograph in front of me again?" But this time, a small smile appeared on his face.

"لأ. بدّي نعْمُل شي مْميّز للْعروس. شو رأْيك تْغنّي بيْن الطّاوْلات وأنا بْصوِّر ردِّةْ فِعِل النّاس؟"

"No. I want to do something special for the bride. What do you think about singing between the tables while I photograph people's reactions?"

"بسّ هيْك بِتْخرْبي الأصول! العريس لازِم..."

"But that breaks tradition! The groom must..."

"العريس مْوافق. وبْتِطْلع أحْلى مِن تحْت الكاميرا."

"The groom agrees. And you'll look better on camera."

غسّان فكّر شْوَيّ. "طيِّب. بسّ بِشرْط: بعِد العِرِس، بِتْفرْجيني الصُّوَر قبِل ما تعْطِيا للْعروس."

Ghassan thought for a moment. "Okay. But on one condition: after the wedding, show me the photos before you give them to the bride."

هنا ستْغْربِت. "ليْه؟"

Hana was surprised. "Why?"

"لِأنّي بدّي شوف العِرِس مِن عْيونِك."

"Because I want to see the wedding through your eyes."

هَيْدي الجِمْلِة خلِّت قلْب هنا يْدِقّ بِسِرْعة، بسّ ما بيِّنِتْلو.

That sentence made Hana's heart beat faster, but she didn't show it.

العِرِس كان مِخْتِلِف عن كِلّ الأعْراس يَلّي صوّرِتا هنا. غسّان تْنقّل بيْن الطّاوْلات، غنّى لِلكْبار ولِلصْغار، والنّاس تْفاعلوا معو بِشكِل عفَوي. هنا صوّرِت كِلّ لحْظة: الضِّحْكات، الدُّموع، الِعْناق، والرّقص.

The wedding was different from all the weddings Hana had photographed. Ghassan moved between tables, sang for the elderly and the young, and people interacted with him spontaneously. Hana captured every moment: the laughter, tears, hugs, and dancing.

بعِد العِرِس، قعدوا بِقهْوِة قريبِة يِتْفرّجوا عَ الصُّوَر.

After the wedding, they sat in a nearby café to look at the photos.

"شو هالْموْهبِة "!قال غسّان وهُوِّ عم يْشوف الصُّوَر. "إنْتي ما عم تْصوْري بسّ، عم تِحْكي قِصّة."

"What talent!" said Ghassan as he looked at the photos. "You're not just photographing, you're telling a story."

"وإنْتَ ما عم بِتْغنّي بسّ، عم تِخْلق ذِكْرَيات."

"And you're not just singing, you're creating memories."

تْطلّعوا بِبعْض، وللْمرّة الأولى حسّوا إنّو في شي عم يِتْغيّر بَيْنُن.

They looked at each other, and for the first time felt that something was changing between them.

"بْتعِرْفي،" قال غسّان، "أنا كِنِت دايْماً مْفكّر إنّو الأعْراس لازِم تْكون بِنفْس الطّريقة. بسّ إنْتي عم تْخلّيني شوف الأُمور بِشكِل تاني."

"You know," said Ghassan, "I always thought weddings had to be done the same way. But you're making me see things differently."

"وأنا كِنْت مْفكّْرة إنّو الأغاني التّْقْليدية قديمِة وبِتْزهِّق. بسّ صَوْتك... بيخلّي كِلّ شي يْصير جْديد."

"And I thought traditional songs were old and boring. But your voice... makes everything sound new."

"عِنْدي حفْلِة الخميس الجاي بِمطْعم البحِر. مِش عِرِس، بسّ حفْلِة عادية. بِتْحبّي تِجي تِسْمعيني؟"

"I have a concert next Thursday at the seaside restaurant. Not a wedding, just a regular concert. Would you like to come listen?"

هنا حسِّت بِفراشات بِقلْبا. "بسّ ما في عِرِس للتّْصْوير!"

Hana felt butterflies in her heart. "But there's no wedding to photograph!"

"ما في عِرِس، بسّ في مَوْعد... إذا بِتْحبّي."

"No wedding, but there's a date... if you'd like."

الحفْلِة كانِت مِخْتِلْفِة عن الأعْراس. غسّان غنّى أغاني حِلْوِة ورايْقة، وهنا قعدِت تِسْمع وتِتْبسّم. بعِد الحفْلِة، مِشْيوا على الكورْنيش.

The concert was different from weddings. Ghassan sang beautiful, quiet songs, and Hana sat listening and smiling. After the concert, they walked along the Corniche.

"ليْه ما بِتْغنّي هيْك بِالْأعْراس؟" سألِت هنا.

"Why don't you sing like this at weddings?" asked Hana.

"بِالأعْراس النّاس بدّا تِسْمع أغاني مْعيّنِة. بسّ بِالْحفْلات... بِقْدر غنّي يَلّي بْحِبّو."

"At weddings, people want to hear certain songs. But at concerts... I can sing what I love."

"وشو بِتْحِبّ تْغنّي؟"

"And what do you love to sing?"

بلّش غسّان يْغنّي بِصوْت واطي غِنِّية قديمِة عن الحُبّ. هنا حسِّت قلْبا عم بيرفْرِف.

Ghassan started singing softly an old love song. Hana felt her heart flutter.

مِن هَيْداك اليوْم، صار كِلّ شي مِخْتِلِف. بِالْأعْراس، صاروا يِتْعاوَنوا مع بعْض. هُوِّ بْيِخْتار أغاني حِلْوِة، وهِيِّ بِتْصوِّر أحْلى اللّحْظات.

From that day, everything became different. At weddings, they started working together. He would choose beautiful songs, and she would capture the best moments.

يوْم الأحد، اتّصلِت فِيا صديقِتا سارة. "بدّي عِرْسي يْكون مْميّز. بِتقْدري تْجيبي غسّان يْغنّي؟"

On Sunday, her friend Sara called. "I want my wedding to be special. Can you get Ghassan to sing?"

هنا ضِحْكِت. "رح إسْألو."

Hana laughed. "I'll ask him."

بعِرِس سارة، غنّى غسّان أجْمل ما عِنْدو. وبِآخر اللّيْل، طلب مِن هنا تِرْقُص معو.

At Sara's wedding, Ghassan sang his best. And at the end of the night, he asked Hana to dance with him.

"بسّ مين رح يْصوِّر؟" سألِت هنا.

"But who will take photos?" asked Hana.

"اليوْم، خلّيكي بسّ عيشي اللّحْظة."

"Today, just live in the moment."

رقصوا سَوا، وتحْت ضوْ القمر، سألا: "شو رأْيك نعْمُل عِرِس خاصّ فينا؟ بسّ هالْمرّة، إنْتي العروس وأنا العريس."

They danced together, and under the moonlight, he asked her, "What do you think about having our own special wedding? But this time, you're the bride and I'm the groom."

هنا بْتسمِت: "بسّ مين رح يْغنّي؟"

Hana smiled, “But who will sing?”

”أنا بْغنّيلِك. ومين رح يْصوِّر؟”

“I’ll sing for you. And who will take photos?”

”في كْتير ناس بْيعِرْفوا يْصوْروا. بسّ ما في حدا بْيِغْنّي مِثْلك.”

“Many people know how to take photos. But no one sings like you.”

صوْت وصورة

"اِوْعى تْخبّْري حدا، بسّ هَيْدي أجْمل صورة شِفْتا بِحَياتي."

هنا سكتِت لحْظة قبِل ما تْردّ على العروس يَلّي قِدّاما. كانِت عم تِتطّلع عَ الشّاشِة الصّْغيرِة بِكاميرْتا - صورة لسِتّ العروس عم تِمْسح دمْعة مِن خدّا وَقِت حفيدِتا عم تِرْقُص مع عريسا. اللّحْظة كانِت عفَويه، والإضاءة مِثاليه، وصوْت غسّان بِالْخلْفية كان عم يْغنّي "يا قمر يا نور عيْني."

"أنا ما صوّْرْتا،" قالِت هنا بِبساطة. "إخْتِك رنا هِيِّ يَلّي مِسْكِت الكاميرا وَقْتا."

العروس فتّحِت عْيونا بْدهْشِة. "رنا؟ بسّ هِيِّ ما بْتعْرِف تْصوِّر!"

"بْتعِرْفي، كِلّ واحد فينا عِنْدو عيْن للْجمال. بسّ في ناس بيخافوا يْعبْروا عن نظْرِتُن. إخْتِك شافِت لحْظة حِلْوِة وصوّرِتا. أنا بسّ علّمْتا كيف تِمْسُك الكاميرا."

"مِتِل ما علّمْتيني كيف إخْتار زاوْيِةْ التّْصوير؟" صوْت رُجولي دافي مِن وَراها.

هنا بْتسمِت وما لْتفتِت. "وإنْتَ مِتِل ما علّمِتْني إسْمع الموسيقى، مِش بسّ سجِّلا يا غسّان."

مِن وَرا العروس، غمز غسّان هنا. صارْلُن سِنْتيْن عم يِشْتِغْلوا سَوا بِأعْراس بَيْروت، وكِلّ مرّة بْيِكْتِشْفوا شي جْديد عن بعْضُن وعن شِغْلُن.

Sound and Image

"Don't tell anyone, but this is the most beautiful photo I've ever seen."

Hana paused before responding to the bride in front of her. She was looking at the small screen of her digital camera – a photo of the bride's grandmother wiping a tear from her cheek while her granddaughter danced with her groom. The moment was spontaneous, the lighting perfect, and Ghassan's voice in the background was singing "Ya Amar Ya Nour Eini" (Oh Moon, Light of My Eyes).

"I didn't take it," Hana said simply. "Your sister Rana held the camera at that moment."

The bride's eyes widened in surprise. "Rana? But she doesn't know how to photograph!"

"You know, everyone has an eye for beauty. But some people are afraid to express their vision. Your sister saw a beautiful moment and captured it. I just taught her how to hold the camera."

"Like how you taught me to choose the right angle?" a warm male voice came from behind her.

Hana smiled without turning around. "And like how you taught me to listen to music, not just record it, Ghassan."

Behind the bride, Ghassan winked at Hana. They had been working together at Beirut weddings for two years, and each time they discovered something new about each other and their professions.

"بْتعِرْفي شو أكْتر شي بْيِعْجِبْني بِشِغْلك؟" سأل غسّان وهِنّي عم يِتْمشّوا بعِد العِرِس. "إنِّك بِتْشوفي الجمال بِمحلّات ما حدا بْيِنْتِبِهْلا. مِش بسّ العروس والعريس..."

"لأ، كمان التّيتا يَلّي عم تْغنّي بِصوْت واطي، والطِّفِل يَلّي نام على كِتِف بيّو، والصّبية يَلّي عم تِضْحك مع صديقِتا..."

"هَيْدا عنجدّ. أنا لمّا بْغنّي، بْحِسّ حالي عم إحْكي قِصّة. وإنْتي بِتْصوْري هالْقِصّة."

وَقْفِت هنا فجْأة. قدامُن، على الكوْرْنيش، كان في عازِف كمان عم يِعْزُف لحِن قديم. الضَّوْ خفيف مِن الأضْوية، الجَوْ رومانْسي كْتير .

"شو؟" سألا.

"ما شي... بسّ... هَيْدي اللّحْظة. حسّيْتا مْميّزة."

غسّان تْطلّع بْعيونا. "طيِّب ليْه ما معِك كاميرْتك هلّأ؟"

"في لحْظات أحْلى نْعيشا مِن دون ما نْصوِّرا."

هزّ راسو. "معِك حقّ. مِتِل الموسيقى. في أغاني بْتِبْقى بِالْقلِب، حتّى لَوْ ما سجّلْناها."

كانوا قاعْدين بِقهْوِة صْغيرِة بِالْجِمّيْزِة، ملفّات الصُّوَر مفْتوحة على لابْتوب هنا، ودفْتر نوتات غسّان على الطّاوْلِة.

"شِفِت هالصّورة؟" سألِت هنا. "لاحظِت كيف العالم بْيِتْفاعل مع صوْتك؟ بِتْحِبّ تْغنّي بيْن النّاس، مِش بسّ عَ المسْرح."

"You know what I love most about your work?" asked Ghassan as they walked after the wedding ended, "That you see beauty in places no one notices. Not just the bride and groom..."

"No, also the grandmother singing softly, the child sleeping on his father's shoulder, the girl laughing with her friend..."

"Exactly that. When I sing, I feel like I'm telling a story. You photograph that story."

Hana suddenly stopped. In front of them, on the Corniche, a violinist was playing an old melody. The dim light from the lanterns was casting shadows on Ghassan's face.

"What?" he asked.

"Nothing... just... this moment. It felt special."

Ghassan looked into her eyes. "Well, why don't you have your camera now?"

"Some moments are better lived than photographed."

He nodded. "You're right. Like music. Some songs stay in the heart, even if we don't record them."

They were sitting in a small café in Gemmayzeh, photo files open on Hana's laptop, and Ghassan's music notes on the table.

"Did you see this photo?" asked Hana. "Did you notice how people react to your voice? You love singing among people, not just on stage."

"وإنْتي بِتْحبّي تْصوْري النّاس على طبيعِتُن، مِش بسّ بوز مدْروس،" رد غسّان. "عِنْدي فِكْرة... بسّ يِمْكِن مجْنونِة."

"قول."

"شو رأْيِك نعْمُل معْرض؟ صُوَر وموسيقى. إنْتي بْتعرْضي أحْلى لحْظات صَوّرْتِيا، وأنا بْغنّي الأغاني كجوّ."

عْيون هنا لمعِت. "معْرض عن الأعْراس؟"

"لأ... معْرض عن اللّحْظات. عن الحُبّ بِكِلّ أشْكالو. الحُبّ يَلّي مِنْشوفو بِالْأعْراس، بيْن الأهِل، بيْن الأصْحاب..."

"... وبيْن المُغنّي والمْصوْرة؟" سألِت هنا بِصوْت واطي.

غسّان سكت شْوَيّ. "بْتعِرْفي؟ مِن أوّل ما شِفْتِك وإنْتي عم تزِعْجيني بِالتُّصْوير، كِنت حاسِس إنّو في شي مِخْتِلِف فيكي. إنْتي ما بِتْشوفي بسّ يلّي قِدّامك. بِتْشوفي القِصّة كِلّا."

"وإنْتَ... إنْتَ ما بِتْغنّي بسّ. بْتِحْكي حْكايِة بِصوْتك. كِلّ غِنِيّة إلا معْنى."

"طيِّب... خلّيْنا نِكْتُب حْكايِتْنا. بسّ هالْمرّة، بدل ما تْصوْرِيا، عيشِيا معي."

بعِد شهِر، كان المعْرض جاهِز. صُوَر هنا على الحيْطان، وغسّان عم يْغنّي بيْن النّاس. بْآخِر اللّيْل، وِقِف غسّان وَسط المعْرض.

"في صورة جْديدِة ما عْرضْناها،" قال للْجُمْهور. على الشّاشة الكْبيرِة، ظهرِت صورة إلو وهُوِّ راكِع قِدّام هنا على الكوْرْنيش.

"And you love photographing people naturally, not just posed shots," Ghassan replied. "I have an idea... but maybe it's crazy."

"Tell me."

"What do you think about doing an exhibition? Photos and music. You display your best captured moments, and I sing the songs that were their backdrop."

Hana's eyes sparkled. "An exhibition about weddings?"

"No... an exhibition about moments. About love in all its forms. The love we see at weddings, between family, between friends..."

"...and between the singer and the photographer?" Hana asked softly.

Ghassan paused. "You know? From the first time I saw you annoying me with your photography, I felt there was something different about you. You don't just see what's in front of you. You see the whole story."

"And you... you don't just sing. You tell a story with your voice. Every song has meaning."

"Well... let's write our story. But this time, instead of photographing it, live it with me."

A month later, the exhibition was ready. Hana's photos on the walls, and Ghassan singing among people. At the end of the night, Ghassan stood in the middle of the exhibition.

"There's a new photo we haven't shown," he told the audience. On the big screen appeared a photo of him kneeling before Hana on the Corniche.

“يِمْكِن أوّل مرّة بِحَياتي، بدّي غنّي مِن دون ما حدا يْصَوِّر. لِأنّو هالمرّة، المْصوْرةْ رح تْكون العروس.”

وبْصوْت دافي، بلّش يْغنّي غِنّيةْ حُبّ قديمِة، وعْيونو ما فارقِت عْيون هنا.

بعِد سِتّةْ شْهور، كان في عِرِس مِخْتِلف بِكْنيسِةْ مار مْخايِل. الِمْصَوْرين كانوا أصْحاب هنا، والمُغنّي كان العريس. بسّ أحْلى لحْظة كانِت لمّا العروس تركِت الكاميرا عَ جنب، ومِسْكِت إيد عريسا، وغنّو سَوا.

“Maybe for the first time in my life, I want to sing without anyone photographing. Because this time, the photographer will be the bride.”

And in a warm voice, he began singing an old love song, his eyes never leaving Hana’s.

Six months later, there was a different wedding at Saint Michael’s Church. The photographers were Hana’s friends, and the singer was the groom. But the most beautiful moment was when the bride put down her camera, took her groom’s hand, and they sang together.

الشِّتي

Winter Rain

On a stormy winter afternoon, when the شِتي *šíti* (rain) pounds Beirut's ancient streets, a traditional قهْوِة *ʔáhwi* (café) becomes an unexpected sanctuary. Inside, where the aroma of fresh coffee mingles with the smoke of water pipes, an unlikely group gathers: a مُهنْدْسِة *muhándsi* (architect) racing to document vanishing heritage, an elderly شوْفور تاكْسي *[choffeur] tēksi* (taxi driver) who once crossed the city's divide, an Armenian جَوْهرْجي *jawhárji* (jeweler) guarding the secrets of his حِرف *ħíraf* (craft), and others whose lives tell the story of a changing city. Through their ذِكْرَيات *zikrayēt* (memories) and حْكايات *ħkēyēt* (stories), we discover how a simple rainstorm might help preserve what luxury buildings and real estate developers threaten to erase from the city's ذاكْرة *zēkra* (memory).

Key Vocabulary

- أسْرار (*asrār*) – secrets
- برِق (*bári?*) – lightning
- حِرَفي (*ɧírafi*) – craftsman
- حيّ (*ɧayy*) – neighborhood
- رِعد (*rá3id*) – thunder
- زبون (*zabūn*) – customer
- عاصْفة (*3āṣfa*) – storm
- هَوى (*háwa*) – wind
- أرْمَني (*?ármani*) – Armenian
- بَلَد (*bálad*) – country, hometown
- تُراث (turās) – heritage
- الْجِمّيْزِة (*-ljimmēzi*) – Gemmayze (neighborhood in Beirut)
- سوق (*sū?*) – market
- صِناعة (*ṣinā3a*) – craft, trade
- فانوس (*fānūs*) – lantern
- مُهَنْدْسِة (*muhándsi*) – engineer/architect

A1

Winter Rain	*-šš íti*	الشِّتي
One Thursday, it rained heavily in Beirut. Rita entered an old café in Gemmayze.	*yōm xamīs, -ššíti nízil ktīr bi-bayrūt. rītta fētit 3ála ʔáhwi ʔadīmi bi-ljimmēzi.*	يوْم خميس، الشِّتي نِزِل كْتير بِبَيْروت. ريتّا فاتِت على قهْوِة قديمِة بِالْجِمّيْزِة.
In the café, she found four people: Ammar the café owner, Abu Fouad the old taxi driver, Bedo the Armenian jeweler, and Jad who returned from Canada.	*bi-lʔáhwi, líʔyit ʔárba3 ʔašxāṣ: 3ammār ṣāɦib ilʔáhwi, u ʔábu fuʔād šōfūr ittēksi -lʔadīm, u bēdu -ljawhárji -lʔármani, u jād yálli rēji3 min kánada.*	بِالْقهْوِة، لِقْيِت أرْبع أشْخاص: عمّار صاحِب القهْوِة، وأبو فُؤاد شوْفور التّاكْسي القديم، وبيْدو الجَوْهرْجي الأرْمني، وجاد يَلّي راجِع مِن كندا.
They drank coffee together and talked about old Beirut. Abu Fouad talked about his taxi, and Bedo talked about the old market.	*šírbu ʔáhwi ma3 ba3ḍ, u ɦíkyu 3an bayrūt ilʔadīmi. ʔábu fuʔād ɦíki 3an ittēksi tába3u, u bēdu ɦíki 3an issūʔ ilʔadīm.*	شِرْبوا قهْوِة مع بعْض، وحِكْيوا عن بَيْروت القديمِة. أبو فُؤاد حِكي عن التّاكْسي تبعو، وبيْدو حِكي عن السّوق القديم.

When the rain let up, they had become friends. They decided to meet every week and tell stories about Beirut.

lámma xaff iššíti, kēnu ṣāru rífʔa. ʔárraru yijtímʒu kill ʔusbūʒ u yíḥku ʔíṣaṣ bayrūt.

لمّا خفّ الشِّتي، كانوا صاروا رِفْقا. قرّروا يِجْتِمْعوا كِلّ أُسْبوع ويِحْكوا قِصص بَيْروت.

A2

Winter Rain	**الشِّتي**
On Thursday, the rain was very heavy in Beirut. The streets became small rivers, and the wind was strong.	يوْم الخميس، الشِّتي كان قوي كْتير بِبَيْروت. الشَّوارِع صارِت أنْهار صْغيرِة، والهَوى قَوي.
In an old café in Gemmayze, Rita took shelter from the rain. Rita is an architect who was photographing old houses in the neighborhood.	في قهْوِة قديمِة بِالجِمّيْزِة، فاتِت ريتّا تِحْتِمي مِن الشِّتي. ريتّا مْهنْدْسِة مِعْمارية، كانِت عم تْصوِّر البْيوت القديمِة بِالْحيّ.
In the café, there were four people: Abu Fouad, a seventy-year-old taxi driver; Bedo, the Armenian uncle who has a jewelry shop in the market; Jad, who returned from Canada to visit Beirut; and the café owner, Ammar.	بِالْقهْوِة، كان في أرْبع أشْخاص: أبو فُؤاد، شوْفور التّاكْسي يَلّي عُمْرو سبْعين سِنِة، وبيْدو العمّ الأرْمني يَلّي عِنْدو محلّ مُجوْهرات بِالسّوق، وجاد يَلّي رِجِع مِن كندا يْزور بَيْروت، وصاحِب القهْوِة، عمّار.
"Coffee's on me," said Ammar. "We'll have to stay here for a while. The street is blocked by rain."	"القهْوِة عليّي،" قال عمّار. "رح نِضْطّر نْضلّ هوْن شْوَيّ. الشّارِع مْسكّر مِن الشِّتي."

They started talking together. Abu Fouad talked about how he used to drive people in his old taxi during the war. Bedo talked about his old shop in the market, and how he learned jewelry-making from his grandfather.	بلّشوا يِحْكوا مع بعْض. أبو فُؤاد خبّر كيف كان يْوصِّل النّاس بِتاكْسيتو القديمِة إيّام الحرِب. بيْدو خبّر عن محلّو القديم بِالسّوق، وكيف تْعلّم صِناعِةْ المُجوْهرات مِن جِدّو.
"What are you doing in Gemmayze?" Jad asked Rita.	"شو عم تعِمْلي بِالْجِمّيْزِة؟" سأل جاد ريتّا.
"I'm photographing the old houses. I'm afraid they'll disappear with time."	"عم صوِّر البْيوت القديمِة. خايْفِة تْضيع مع الوَقِت."
"I've lived in this neighborhood for fifty years," said Bedo. "Every house has a story."	"أنا عِشْت بِهالْحيّ مِن خمْسين سِنِة،" قال بيْدو. "كِلّ بيْت عِنْدو قِصّة."
The rain kept falling heavily, and they kept talking. When the rain lightened, they felt they had become friends.	الشِّتي ضلّ يِنْزل بِقُوِّة، وهِنّي ضلّوا يِحْكوا. لمّا خفّ الشِّتي، حسّوا إنُّن صاروا أصْحاب.
"We must meet again," said Rita. "I now have new friends who know old Beirut's history."	"لازِم نِلْتِقي مرّة تانْيِة،" قالِت ريتّا. "صار عِنْدي رِفْقا جْداد بْيعِرْفوا تاريخ بَيْروت القديمِة."

الشِّتي

Winter Rain

ما حدا بِبَيْروت شاف هيْك شِتي مِن سْنين طَويلِة. السّما كانِت سَوْدا، والِغْيوم تْقيلِة، والرّيح عم بِتْهِزّ أغْصان الشّجر القديمِة بِشوارِع الجِمّيْزِة. شهِر كانون، وبَيْروت عم تِغْرق.

No one in Beirut had seen such rain in many years. The sky was black, the clouds heavy, and the wind was shaking the old tree branches in Gemmayze's streets. It was December, and Beirut was drowning.

ريتّا كانِت عم تْصوِّر بيْت قديم لمّا بلّشِت الشّتْوة الِكْبيرِة تِنْزل. حطِّت الكاميرا بِشنْطِتا وركضِت تِحْتِمي. أقْرب محلّ كان "قهْوِةْ زمان"، قهْوِة عتيقة بِواجْهِةْ حجر وشْبابيك قناطِر.

Rita was photographing an old house when the large raindrops began to fall. She put her camera in her bag and ran for shelter. The nearest place was "Café Zaman," an ancient café with a stone facade and arched windows.

"أهْلا وسهْلا!" رحّب فِيا عمّار، صاحِب القهْوِة. كان رِجّال بِعُمِر الخمْسين، وِجّو بشوش ومرْيول أزْرق عْليْه رسْمِةْ فِنْجان قهْوِة. "في عِنّا ضْيوف كْتار اليوْم. الشِّتي جمعْنا."

"Welcome!" greeted Ammar, the café owner. He was a man in his fifties, with a cheerful face and a blue apron decorated with a coffee cup design. "We have many guests today. The rain has brought us together."

كان في أرْبع زبايِن: أبو فُؤاد، شوْفور تاكْسي خِتْيار قاعِد حدّ الشِّباك، عم يْدخِّن أرْجيلِة ويْراقِب الشِّتي. وبيْدو أفاديشْيان، جَوْهرْجي أرْمني

مغْروف بِالسّوق، عم يِلْعب طاوْلِة مع جاد، شبّ لِبْناني راجِع مِن كندا.

There were four customers: Abu Fouad, an elderly taxi driver sitting by the window, smoking a water pipe and watching the rain; Bedo Avadisian, a well-known Armenian jeweler from the market, playing backgammon with Jad, a Lebanese man back from Canada.

"تْفضّلي، القهْوِة عْليّي،" قال عمّار. "الجّوّ هيْك بْيِطّْلُب قهْوِة سادة."

"Please, coffee's on me," said Ammar. "This weather calls for black coffee."

برّا، صوْت الرّعد صار أقْوى. الشّارِع تْحوّل لنهْر صْغير، والهَوى صار يْصفْر بيْن البْيوت القديمِة.

Outside, the thunder grew louder. The street turned into a small river, and the wind whistled between the old houses.

"عنْجدّ هالجوْ بيذكِّرْني بِشِتي سِنِة ٨٧،" قال أبو فُؤاد. "وَقْتا كِنِت بعِدْني بِشْتِغِل بِالتّاكْسي. ضلّيْت شي خمْس ساعات واقِف بِالطّريق."

"This weather really reminds me of the winter of '87," said Abu Fouad. "I was still driving my taxi then. I was stuck on the road for about five hours."

"إنْتَ بِتْسوق تاكْسي مِن زمان؟" سألِت ريتّا.

"Have you been a taxi driver for long?" asked Rita.

"مِن عُمْر العِشْرين. شِفت كِلّ شي بِهالْمدينِة. إيّام الحرِب، كِنِت وَصِّل النّاس مِن الشّرْقية للْغرْبية. التّاكسي الأصْفر كان يِمْرُق مِن كِلّ الحَواجِز."

"Since I was twenty. I've seen everything in this city. During the war, I used to take people from East to West. The yellow taxi could pass through all checkpoints."

"صحّ،" قال بيْدو. "كان يْجيب لعِنْدي بْضاعة مِن برّا السّوق. بْتعِرْفي يا آنْسِة، محلّ المُجوْهرات تبعي كان لجِدّي. مِن إيّام ما كان السّوق كِلّو خِيَم وبسْطات."

"True," said Bedo. "He used to bring me merchandise from outside the market. You know, miss, my jewelry shop belonged to my grandfather. From the days when the market was all tents and stalls."

"وإنْتي شو عم تعِمْلي بهالشِّتي؟" سأل جاد ريتّا.

"And what are you doing in this rain?" Jad asked Rita.

"أنا مْهنْدْسِة مِعْمارية. عم وثِّق البْيوت التُّراثية بِالْجِمّيْزِة قبل ما تِخْتِفي. كِلّ أُسْبوع في بيْت عم يِنْهدّ."

"I'm an architect. I'm documenting the heritage houses in Gemmayze before they disappear. Every week another house is demolished."

"معِك حقّ،" قال جاد. "أنا ترْكت بَيْروت مِن عشْر سْنين. كِلّ ما بِرْجع بلاقِيا تْغيّرِت. حتّى بيْت سِتّي القديم صار بِرِج."

"You're right," said Jad. "I left Beirut ten years ago. Every time I return, I find it changed. Even my grandmother's old house is now a tower."

برّا، الشِّتي ضلّ يِنْزل بِقُوِّة. عمّار جاب صيْنيِةْ قهْوِة وصحِن بِقْلاوة. "هَيْدا الجوّ بدّو حكي وذِكْرَيات."

Outside, the rain kept falling heavily. Ammar brought a tray of coffee and a plate of baklava. "This weather is made for stories and memories."

"بْتعِرْفوا،" قال بيْدو، "المحلّ يَلّي حضِرْتِك عم تْصوْري حدّو، كان بيْت صديقي أنْطون. يِمْكِن أَحْسن صايِغ دهب بِالْمنْطقة..."

"You know," said Bedo, "the shop you were photographing next door used to be my friend Anton's house. Perhaps the best goldsmith in the area..."

"حْكيلْنا عن أنْطونْ،" قالِت ريتّا، وهِيِّ عم تِطلِّع الكاميرا مِن شنْطِتا.

"Tell us about Anton," said Rita, taking her camera out of her bag.

تْنهّد بيْدو: "كان عِنْدو محلّ صْغير، بسّ شِغْلو كان فنّ. تعلّم الصِّناعة مِن أهْلو بِحلب. جاب معو كِلّ أدَواتو لمّا هاجر على بَيْروت. كِنّا نِقْعُد آخِر اللّيْل نْصمِّم مُجوْهرات مع بعْض."

Bedo sighed, "He had a small shop, but his work was art. He learned the craft from his family in Aleppo. He brought all his tools with him when he immigrated to Beirut. We used to sit late into the night designing jewelry together."

"ويْن صار؟" سأل جاد.

"What happened to him?" asked Jad.

"سافر على أميْركا بِالتّْمانينات. وْلادو ما حبّوا يِتْعلّموا المِهْنِة. هيْك عم بِتْضيع الحِرف القديمِة."

"He left for America in the eighties. His children didn't want to learn the trade. That's how the old crafts are disappearing."

قاطعُن صوْت رعِد قَوي. ضوِّت السّما كِلّا، وفجْأة طِفْيِت الكهْربا.

A loud thunder interrupted them. The whole sky lit up, and suddenly the electricity went out.

"ما تِعْتلوا همّ!" قال عمّار. "عِنْدي شمِع وفانوس قديم."

"Don't worry!" called Ammar. "I have candles and an old lantern."

ضوّ الفانوس عطى القهْوِة جوّ غريب. الضّوّ الخفيف خلّا الوْجوهْ تْبيِّن أقْرب لبعْضا، والحكي صار أعْمق.

The lantern's light gave the café a strange atmosphere. The dim light made faces appear closer to each other, and the conversation grew deeper.

أبو فُؤاد خبّر عن بَيْروت القديمِة، عن النّاس يَلّي كان يْوصِّلُن بِتاكْسيتو. "كِلّ راكِب عِنْدو قِصّة. كِنِت مِتِل كْتاب مِتْنقِّل."

Abu Fouad talked about old Beirut, about the people he used to drive in his taxi. "Every passenger had a story. I was like a moving book."

جاد حِكي كيف ترك بَيْروت بعِد الحرِب: "بسّ القلِب ما بْيِنْسى. كِلّ ليْلِة بِبيْتي عَ الدّوْرة مِن زمان كِنْت إسْمع صوْت البحِر."

Jad talked about how he left Beirut after the war, "But the heart never forgets. Every night in my house in Dora, I could hear the sound of the sea."

ريتّا صارِت تْسجِّل كِلّ شي على تِلِفونا. "هَيْدي القِصص لازِم تِنْحفظ،" قالِت. "كِلّ واحد فيكُن عِنْدو جِزِء مِن تاريخ المدينِة."

Rita started recording everything on her phone. "These stories must be preserved," she said. "Each of you has a piece of the city's history."

الشِّتي خفّ شْوَيّ شْوَيّ. الكهْربا رِجْعِت، وصوْت الرّعِد صار بْعيد.

The rain gradually lessened. The electricity came back, and the sound of thunder became distant.

"بُكْرا في شمِس،" قال عمّار. "بسّ رح نِتْذكّر هالنّْهار."

“Tomorrow there will be sun,” said Ammar. “But we’ll remember this day.”

تْبادلوا أرْقام التِّلفونات. ريتّا وعدِت إنّا تْجيب صُوَر البْيوت القديمِة يَلّي صوّرِتا. بيْدو قال بدّو يْفرْجِيا على صُوَر قديمِة للسّوق. وجاد قرّر يْأجِّل سفرو كم يوْم، بدّو يِسْمع قِصص أكْتر.

They exchanged phone numbers. Rita promised to bring photos of the old houses she had photographed. Bedo said he would show her old pictures of the market. And Jad decided to postpone his trip for a few days, wanting to hear more stories.

“بْتعِرْفي شو؟” قال أبو فُؤاد لريتّا وهِيِّ عم تِمْشي. “بَيْروت مِتِل هالشِّتي. مهْما شْتدِّت العاصْفِة، بِتْخِفّ وبْتِرْجع الشّمِس تْضوّي.”

“You know what?” Abu Fouad said to Rita as she was walking away. “Beirut is like this rain. No matter how strong the storm gets, it eases, and the sun comes back to shine.”

الشِّتي

بَيْروت ما بْتشتّي مِتِل باقي المُدُن. شِتِيا بْيِشْبها: مِتْقلِّب، عنيد، وأَوْقات حنون. هالْخميس، المدينِة قرّرِت تِفْتح سماها على آخِرا. الغْيوم السَّوْدا تجمّعِت مِن الصُّبُح، والرّيح يَلّي جاي مِن البحِر حِمْلِت معا ريحِةْ شِتي ما نْشمِّت مِن سْنين.

ريتّا وَقّفِت قِدّام بيْت مِن إيّام الإنْتِداب الفرنْسي، كاميرْتا عم تِرْجُف بإيدا مِن البرِد. كانِت عم بِتْحاوِل تْصوِّر النّقْشِة فوْق الشِّباك - تفاصيل دقيقة مِن حجر رمْلي، بْتِحْكي قِصّةْ عيْلِة عاشِت هوْن مِن مية سِنِة. بُكْرا، يِمْكِن البيْت ما عاد يْكون مَوْجود. شِرْكات العقارات عم تِشْتِري كِلّ شي، وأصْحاب البْيوت القديمِة عم يِسْتسِلْموا للْإغْراءات، واحد وَرا التّاني.

نُقْطِةْ شِتي وَقعِت على عدسِةْ الكاميرا. وبعْدا نُقْطة تانْيِة. وفجْأة، نْفتحِت السّما. ريتّا ركضِت تْنبِّش على ملْجأ، شعْرا الأسْوَد صار يْنقِّط ميّ، وصُبّاطا الجِلِد تْبلّل. بيْن البْيوت العتيقة، لمحِت آرمِةْ خشب قديمِة: "قهْوِةْ زمان".

القهْوِة كانِت مِتِل عِلْبِةْ زمن محْفوظة مِن إيّام بَيْروت القديمِة. حيْطان حجر رمْلي مِصْفر، السّقِف عالي مع مرْوَحة خشب عتيقة، وطاوْلاتا مِن رْخام مْجزّع. ريحِةْ القهْوِة المطْحونِة طازة خْتلطِت مع ريحِةْ الأرْجيلِة وخشب الصُّنوبر القديم.

"يا مِيةْ هلا!" رحّب فِيا عمّار، صاحِب القهْوِة. كان رِجّال طَويل، ضْعيف، بِشعْر أبْيَض كْتاف وعْيون خضْرا بْتِضْحك قبِل شْفافو. "فوتي، فوتي. هلّأ بيصير عِنّا حفْلِة مِن هالشِّتي."

Winter Rain

Beirut doesn't rain like other cities. Its rain resembles it: temperamental, stubborn, and sometimes tender. This Thursday, the city decided to open its sky completely. Black clouds gathered since morning, and the wind coming from the sea carried with it the scent of rain not smelled in years.

Rita stood before a house from the French Mandate period, her camera trembling in her hand from the cold. She was trying to photograph the carving above the window – intricate details in sandstone, telling the story of a family who lived here a hundred years ago. Tomorrow, the house might no longer exist. Real estate companies are buying everything, and owners of old houses are surrendering to temptations, one after another.

A raindrop fell on the camera lens. Then another. Suddenly, the sky opened up. Rita ran looking for shelter, her black hair dripping water, her leather shoes soaked. Among the ancient houses, she spotted an old wooden sign, "Café Zaman" (Time's Café).

The café was like a time capsule preserved from old Beirut. Its walls were of yellowed sandstone, its ceiling high with antique wooden fans, and its tables made of veined marble. The smell of freshly ground coffee mixed with the scent of water pipe and old pine wood.

"Welcome, welcome!" greeted Ammar, the café owner. He was a tall, thin man, with thick white hair and green eyes that laughed before his lips did. "Come in, come in. We're about to have a party in this rain."

كان في كم زْبون مِتْفرْقين بِالْقهْوة. بِالزّاوْيِة، حدّ الشِّباك القنْطرة، قعد أبو فُؤاد، شوْفور تاكْسي كْبير بِالْعُمِر. كان عم يْدخِّن أرْجيلْتو بِبُطِء، عْيونو السّود الِصّْغيرِة عم تْراقِب الشِّتي مِن وَرا عْوَيْناتو. على طاوْلِة قريبِة، بيْدو أفاديسْيان، جَوْهرْجي معْروف بِالسّوق، كان مِنْشِغِل بِلِعْبِةْ طاوْلِة مع شبّ بِعُمْر التّْلاتين - جاد، يَلّي مْبيّن مِن لِهجْتو إنّو عايِش برّا البلد.

"بدِّك فِنْجان قهْوِة؟" سأل عمّار وهُوِّ عم يِمْسح طاوْلِةْ رْخام نْضيفِة. "القهْوِة عَ البيْت. هيْك شِتي بدّو رِفْقة وقهْوِة سادة."

رعِد قوي هزّ شْبابيك القهْوِة. الشِّتي صار يْدِقّ على القْزاز القديم مِتِل طبْلِة صْغيرِة، والرّيح صارِت تْصفِّر بيْن البِنايات.

"آخ يا هالشِّتي،" تْنهّد أبو فُؤاد. "بيذكِّرْني بِشِتي سِنِةْ ٨٧. كِنِت بعِدْني شبّ صْغير، بسّ التّاكْسي كان رْفيقي. ضلّيْت خمْس ساعات واقِف بِمنْطقِةْ الحمْرا. النّاس يَلّي ما قِدْروا يِرْجعوا عَ بْيوتُن صاروا يِرْكبوا معي، وأنا صِرِت إسْمع قِصصُن."

"إنْتَ مِن زمان شوْفور تاكْسي؟" سألِت ريتّا، وهِيِّ عم تْنفِّض الميّ عن شعْرا.

"مِن عُمْر العِشْرين. يَعْني شي خمْسين سِنِة. شِفِت كِلّ شي بِهالمدينة. إيّام الحرِب، التّاكْسي الأصْفر كان الوَحيد يَلّي بْيِقْدر يِمْرق بيْن كِلّ الحواجِز. كِنِت وصِّل النّاس مِن الشّرْقية للْغرْبية. ما حدا كان يْوقِّف تاكْسي صفْرا. كان عِنْدي جَواز مُرور خاصّ."

بيْدو ترك طاوْلِةْ الزّهِر وقرّب مِن طاوْلِتْن. "صحّ كلامو. كان يْجيبْلي بْضاعة مِن برّا السّوق. بْتعِرْفي يا آنْسِة، سوق الصّاغة كان عالم تاني. كِلّ دِكّان عِنْدو قُصّة، كِلّ حِرفي عِنْدو سِرّ."

There were several customers scattered in the café. In the corner, near the arched window, sat Abu Fouad, an elderly taxi driver. He was slowly smoking his water pipe, his small black eyes watching the rain from behind his glasses. At a nearby table, Bedo Avadisian, a well-known jeweler from the market, was absorbed in a backgammon game with a man in his thirties – Jad, whose accent revealed he lived abroad.

"Would you like a cup of coffee?" asked Ammar while wiping a clean marble table. "Coffee's on the house. This kind of rain calls for company and black coffee."

Strong thunder shook the café's windows. The rain began hitting the old glass like small drums, and the wind started whistling between the buildings.

"Ah, this rain," sighed Abu Fouad. "Reminds me of the winter of '87. I was still a young man, but the taxi was my companion. I stayed stuck for five hours in the Hamra area. People who couldn't get home started riding with me, and I started hearing their stories."

"Have you been a taxi driver for long?" asked Rita, shaking water from her hair.

"Since I was twenty. That's about fifty years. I've seen everything in this city. During the war, the yellow taxi was the only one that could pass through all checkpoints. I used to take people from East to West. No one would stop a yellow taxi. I had a special pass."

Bedo left the backgammon table and moved over to their table. "He's right. He used to bring me merchandise from outside the market. You know, miss, the jewelry market was a different world. Every shop had a story, every craftsman had a secret."

"حْكيلي عن السّوق،" قالِت ريتّا، وهِيِّ عم تْطلِّع دفْتر صْغير مِن شنْطِتا.

عْيون بيْدو لمعِت: "محلّ المُجوْهرات تبعي وْرِتّو عن جِدّي. هُوّي كمان وِرْتو عن جدّو. العيْلِة جابِت الصِّنْعة معا مِن أرْمينيا. كان عِنّا صنْدوق خشب عتيق، في كِلّ أدَوات الصِّياغة: ميزان دهب صْغير، مِنْقاش فِضّة، وقَوالِب نْحاس. الصّنْدوق بعْدو مَوْجود بِالدِّكان، بسّ ما حدا بْيِسْتعِمْلو. اليوْم كِلّ شي صار آلات وكومْبيوتِر."

"وإنْتي شو عم تعِمْلي بِهالشّتي؟" سأل جاد ريتّا.

"أنا مْهنْدْسِة مِعْمارِيّة وباحْثِة. عم وثِّق البْيوت التُّراثية بِالْجِمّيْزِة قبل ما تِخْتِفي. كِلّ بيْت بِمْشي حدّو بْحِسّ حالي عم بِخْسر كنِز. كِلّ حجر في قُصّة، كِلّ شِبّاك إلو حْكايِة."

"معِك حقّ،" تْنهّد جاد. "أنا تركت بَيْروت مِن عشْر سْنين، رِحت عَ كندا. صِرت مُدير شِرْكِة برْمجة هوْنيك. بسّ كِلّ ما بِرْجع، بْحِسّ المدينِة عم بِتْضيع مِنّي. حتّى بيْت سِتّي بِالْجِمّيْزِة صار بُرِج."

برّا، الشِّتي زْداد. صوْت الرّعِد قرّب، والبرق صار يْضوّي السّما كِلّ شْوَيّ. عمّار جاب صينِيِّة قهْوِة وصحِن بِقْلاوِة طازة.

"عِنْدي حْكايِة،" قال أبو فُؤاد. "مرّة، بْعِز الحرب، إجِتْني طلبِيِّة توصيل عروس مِن الأشْرفية للْحمْرا. العروس كانِت لابْسِة فِسْتانا الأبْيَض، وأهْلا رافْضين يْأجْلوا العِرِس بِسبب القصِف. قطعْنا الطّريق بْنُص ساعة. صارِت أشْهر عروس بِبَيْروت - العروس يَلّي قطعِت خطّ التّماس بِتاكْسي صفْرا."

"Tell me about the market," said Rita, taking out a small notebook from her bag.

Bedo's eyes sparkled, "I inherited my jewelry shop from my grandfather. He also inherited it from his grandfather. The family brought the craft with them from Armenia. We had an antique wooden box containing all the goldsmith's tools: a small gold scale, silver tweezers, and copper molds. The box is still in the shop, but no one uses it. Today everything is machines and computers."

"And what are you doing in this rain?" Jad asked Rita.

"I'm an architect and researcher. I'm documenting the heritage houses in Gemmayze before they disappear. With every house I walk by, I feel like I'm losing a treasure. Every stone has a story, every window has a tale."

"You're right," Jad sighed. "I left Beirut ten years ago, went to Canada. I became a software company manager there. But every time I return, I feel the city slipping away from me. Even my grandmother's house in Gemmayze has become a tower."

Outside, the rain intensified. The thunder drew closer, and lightning began illuminating the sky frequently. Ammar brought a tray of coffee and a plate of fresh baklava.

"I have a story," said Abu Fouad. "Once, at the height of the war, I got a request to drive a bride from Achrafieh to Hamra. The bride was wearing her white dress, and her family refused to postpone the wedding because of the shelling. We crossed the road in half an hour. She became the most famous bride in Beirut – the bride who crossed the demarcation line in a yellow taxi."

فجأة، طُفْيِت الكهْربا. القهْوِة غِرْقِت بِالْعتْمِة، بسّ عمّار كان جاهِز. طلّع فانوس كاز قديم وشمِع. ضوّ الفانوس وخلّا القهْوِة تِرْجع لإيّام زمان.

"بْتعِرْفوا،" قال بيْدو، "هَيْدي القهْوِة كان مُلْتقى كِلّ الحِرفِيّين. كِلّ مسا، بعِد ما نْسكِّر دْكاكينّا، كِنّا نِجْتِمِع هوْن. النّجار حدّ الصّايِغ، والخِيّاط حدّ الحِدّاد. كِنّا نِحْكي بِالصُّنْعة، ونِتْشارك الأسْرار."

"وأنا كِنِت إسْمع كِلّ شي،" ضِحِك عمّار. "هالطّاوْلِة يَلّي إنْتو قاعْدين عْلَيا، مِن خمْسين سِنِة وهِيِّ عم تِسْمع أسْرار بَيْروت."

ريتّا فتحِت تِلِفونا وبلّشِت تْسجِّل. "هَيْدي مِش مُجرّد حْكايات. هَيْدي تاريخ المدينِة عم يِحْكي."

"صحّ،" قال جاد. "بْتعِرْفوا شو أكْتر شي بيوَجِّعْني؟ إنّو وْلادي ما رح يعِرْفوا هالبْيروت. عِنْدي بِنِت عُمْرا سبْع سْنين، كِلّ ما بْخبِّرا عن المدينِة القديمِة، بْتِسْألْني: ويْن هِيِّ؟"

ضوّ البرِق نوّر القهْوِة للحْظة. بيْدو مسك مسْبحْتو القديمِة وبلّش يِلْعب فِيا . "بْتعِرْفي يا بِنْتي، كِلّ ما بْشوف برِج جْديد عم يِطْلع، بِتْذكّر أنْطوْن."

"مين أنْطون؟" سألِت ريتّا.

"أنْطوْن كان أحْسن صايِغ دهب بِالسّوق. تْعلّم الصُّنْعة مِن عيْلتو بِحلب. جاب معو لبَيْروت صنْدوق أدَوات عُمْرو مية سِنِة. كان يِقْعُد ساعات يِشْتِغِل على قُطْعة وِحْدِة، تيِطْلع الشِّغِل مِتِل التّحْفِة. كِنّا نِسْهر مع بعْض نْصمِّم مُجوْهرات. هُوّي كان يِرْسُم وأنا كِنِت نفِّذ. كِلّ قِطْعة إلا قِصّة."

Suddenly, the electricity went out. The café plunged into darkness, but Ammar was ready. He brought out an old kerosene lantern and candles. The lantern's dim light transported the café back to old times.

"You know," said Bedo, "this café was the meeting point for all craftsmen. Every evening, after closing our shops, we would gather here. The carpenter next to the goldsmith, the tailor next to the blacksmith. We would talk about our crafts, share secrets."

"And I would hear everything," Ammar laughed. "This table you're sitting at has been listening to Beirut's secrets for fifty years."

Rita opened her phone and started recording. "These aren't just stories. This is the city's history speaking."

"True," said Jad. "You know what hurts me the most? That my children will never know this Beirut. I have a seven-year-old daughter, and whenever I tell her about the old city, she asks me: where is it?"

Lightning illuminated the café for a moment. Bedo held his old prayer beads and began playing with them slowly. "You know, my daughter, every time I see a new tower going up, I remember Anton."

"Who's Anton?" asked Rita.

"Anton was the best goldsmith in the market. He learned the craft from his family in Aleppo. He brought to Beirut a toolbox that was a hundred years old. He would spend hours working on a single piece until it came out like a masterpiece. We used to stay up late designing jewelry together. He would draw, and I would execute. Every piece had a story."

"وشو صار معو؟" سأل عمّار.

"سافر عَ أميْرْكا بِالتِّمانينات. وْلادو ما حبّوا يِتْعلّموا الصُّنْعة. آخِر مرّة شِفْتو، عطاني نُصّ أدواتو. قلّي: 'خلِّيْن عِنْدك، هونيْك ما في حدا بْيِفْهم قيمِتْن.'"

الصّمِت عمّ لِلحْظات. الشِّتي خفّ شْوَيّ، وصار صَوْتو مِتِل موسيقى هادْيِة.

"طيِّب ليْش ما مْنعْمُل شي؟" قالِت ريتّا فجْأة. "ليْش ما مِنْوَثِّق كِلّ هالْقِصص؟ كِلّ واحد مِنْكُن عِنْدو جزء مِن روح المدينِة."

"شو يَعْني؟" سأل جاد.

"يَعْني... أنا عِنْدي الصُّوَر، وعم سِجِّل الحكي. بيْدو عِنْدو تاريخ السّوق. وأبو فُؤاد عِنْدو ذِكْريات الشَّوارِع. ليْش ما مْنِجْمع كِلّ هالشّي؟"

"مِتِل متْحف صْغير؟" سأل عمّار.

"أكْتر مِن هيْك. مِتِل أرْشيف حيّ. مْنِحْكي قُصص النّاس والبْيوت والحِرف. مِش بسّ صُوَر وذِكْريات، كمان الأصْوات والرِّوايات."

بيْدو بْتسم: "بْجيب صُوَر السّوق القديمِة. وكمان مُمْكِن نعْمِل معرْض للأدَوات القديمِة."

"وأنا عِنْدي يوْميات مِن إيّام الحرِب،" قال أبو فُؤاد. "كِنت كِلّ يوْم إكْتُب شو بيصير معي بِالتّاكْسي."

"وهالْقهْوِة مُمْكِن تْكون المرْكز،" قال عمّار. "مرْكز ذاكْرِةْ المدينِة."

"What happened to him?" asked Ammar.

"He left for America in the eighties. His children didn't want to learn the craft. The last time I saw him, he gave me half his tools. He told me: 'Keep them with you, over there no one understands their value.'"

Silence fell for a few moments. The rain had lightened, and its sound became like soft music.

"Well, why don't we do something?" Rita suddenly said. "Why don't we document all these stories? Each of you has a piece of the city's soul."

"What do you mean?" asked Jad.

"I mean... I have the photos, and I'm recording the conversations. Bedo has the market's history. And Abu Fouad has memories of the streets. Why don't we collect all of this?"

"Like a small museum?" asked Ammar.

"More than that. Like a living archive. We tell the stories of people, houses, and crafts. Not just photos and memories, but also voices and narratives."

Bedo smiled, "I'll bring photos of the old market. And we could also display the old tools."

"And I have diaries from the war days," said Abu Fouad. "I used to write down everything that happened to me in the taxi each day."

"And this café could be the center," said Ammar. "The city's memory center."

الشِّتي خفّ أكْتر. الكهْربا رِجْعِت، وصوْت الرِّعِد صار بْعيد.

"بُكْرا في شمِس،" قال عمّار وهُوِّ عم يْطفّي الفانوس. "بسّ هالنّْهار رح يْضلّ بِالذّاكْرة."

تْبادلوا أرْقام التِّلِفونات. ريتّا وعدِت تْجيب الصُّوَر الأُسْبوع الجايّ. بِيْدو قال بدّو يْدوِّر عَ الصّنْدوق العتيق. جاد قرّر يْأجِّل سفرو أُسْبوع، بدّو يْساعِد بِالْفِكْرة.

وَقِت فلِّت ريتّا، كانِت نُقط الشِّتي الأخيرة عم تِلْمع تحِت ضوْ الشّوارِع مِتِل دْموع فرح. حسِّت إنّو اليوْم، الشِّتي ما جمع بسّ غُربا بِقهْوِة قديمِة. جمع حْكايات مدينِة ما بدّا تْموت.

The rain lessened further. The electricity returned, and the sound of thunder became distant.

"Tomorrow there will be sun," said Ammar as he extinguished the lantern. "But this day will remain in memory."

They exchanged phone numbers. Rita promised to bring the photos next week. Bedo said he would look for the old box. Jad decided to postpone his trip for a week, wanting to help with the idea.

When Rita left, the last raindrops were glistening under the street lights like tears of joy. She felt that today, the rain hadn't just brought strangers together in an old café. It had gathered the stories of a city that refuses to die.

www.ingramcontent.com/pod-product-compliance
Lightning Source LLC
Chambersburg PA
CBHW071516120626
46550CB00006B/2249
* 9 7 8 1 9 6 2 7 5 2 0 8 4 *